VOICES FROM
THE DEXTER PULPIT

VOICES
FROM THE
DEXTER PULPIT

EDITED AND WITH AN INTRODUCTION
BY MICHAEL THURMAN

FOREWORD BY THE LATE DR. LEON SULLIVAN

NEWSOUTH BOOKS
Montgomery | Louisville

NewSouth Books
P.O. Box 1588
Montgomery, AL 36104

ISBN-13: 978-1-60306-031-8
ISBN-10: 1-60306-031-6

Library of Congress Cataloging-in-Publicaion Data
Voices from the Dexter Puplit / edited and with an introduction by Michael Thurman.
p.cm.
Includes index.

1. Dexter King Memorial Baptist Church (Montgomery, Ala.)—History—20th century.
2. Montgomery (Ala.)—Church History—20th century. 3. Sermons, American—
African American authors. 4. African Americans—Civil Rights—Sermons. 5. African
American Baptists—Sermons. 6. Sermons, American—20th century. I. Thurman,
Michael, 1961–
BX6480.A28 V65 2001
252'.06135—dc21

Design by Randall Williams
Printed in the United States of America

To all of the pastors who graced the Dexter pulpit over the last one hundred and twenty-three years, and to all of the Dexterites who were challenged by the messages of these extraordinary servants of God, and last of all to my family, my mother and father and my faithful wife Pat and Tanerica and Jonathan.

Contents

Foreword

BY DR. LEON SULLIVAN

There is a deep appreciation for places of historical significance! Only a few places can command more attention than the Dexter Avenue King Memorial Baptist Church in Montgomery, Alabama, pastored by Martin Luther King, Jr. from 1954 until 1960. It was from this pulpit and his involvement with the larger community that he launched a movement which ultimately touched the world.

Voices from the Dexter Pulpit brings together the six living pastors who have served the Dexter Avenue King Memorial Baptist Church since 1960 and a sermon each from Vernon Johns and Martin Luther King, Jr. These men have labored in the vineyards of God in an attempt to capture the vision which God gave them for this great church. In these sermons can be found a challenge to every citizen of the world to shoulder the task of making the world a better place to live. The power of the African-American pulpit has been unprecedented in its ability to move people to action, and because of its detachment from the larger community it has enjoyed a sense of freedom that few institutions within the African-American community have enjoyed.

Dexter has influenced my life over the years, in that as a child growing up in Charleston, West Virginia, the Reverend Vernon Johns was my first pastor. Later during the turbulent sixties I had an opportunity to advise Martin Luther King, Jr., on matters regarding selective patronage and in the development of economic development strategies, which resulted in Operation Breadbasket. Johns and King shared Dexter as a common experience in their lives. Who would have dreamed that one would follow the other?

I continue to be confident that the African-American church can be a vehicle for change in society. From the pulpit of Zion Baptist Church, my former church in Philadelphia, we mobilized people to purchase apartment buildings and a shopping center, we started the Opportunities Industrialization Center (O.I.C.), and later we launched the International Foundation for Education and Self-Help (IFESH). This represents one church!

There is no telling what can be done if churches would partner in joint ventures and pool their resources and energies. A little more than a year ago, the Reverend Michael Thurman, the editor of this book, came to visit me at the IFESH office in Phoenix. He asked me what I foresaw as the relevance of the African-American church in the future, and my response was that as long as there is a need for the Jewish synagogue there will be a need for the African-American church. Without the Jewish synagogue there is no Jewish community, for Jewish life revolves around the synagogue. Thus, the same with the African-American community—black life finds at its center the black church.

The task remains for churches like Dexter and scores of others to provide a prescriptive program to address the needs of our people and provide economic and social uplift. This massive task will require the best of our intellectual talents and business savvy. We must expend the necessary energies because our salvation lies within the ark of the black church.

Preface

The Dexter Avenue King Memorial Baptist Church is an active, living church. It also happens to be one of the great landmarks of America. It is truly a humbling, awesome experience to pastor this church, a reality which is not lost on its discerning members and visitors. Many have asked me, "What is it like to stand in that historic pulpit?" "What is it like to pastor in that edifice from which some of the most riveting of socio-economic justice has emanated?" This book is an opportunity to give some insight to those questions, but its purpose goes even deeper.

In November 1996, as I responded to the challenge to lead this great congregation, I immediately sensed the heavy burden that I had undertaken. I had grown up in Montgomery and had known many Dexter people all of my life in various capacities, but I realized that I did not know Dexter as an institution. As students of corporate cultures will readily agree, every organization has its own unique flavor, and Dexter was no exception. Having read Taylor Branch's *Parting The Waters* not once, but twice, I knew that this would be no easy journey. I also knew that with God's help I could not fail.

Like General Patton surveying the battlefields of ancient wars, I would sometimes sit in the pews of Dexter's stately sanctuary and contemplate the voices of the great preachers who have graced its pulpit in the past, men like Mordecai Johnson, Benjamin E. Mays, Gardner Taylor, Leon Sullivan, Wyatt T. Walker, and, of course the former pastors Vernon Johns and Martin Luther King, Jr.

Even more intriguing to me was the gallery of "Photos of Our Former Pastors" located on the west wall of the church basement, that historic space where on December 5, 1955, the 26-year-old King was elected president of the newly organized Montgomery Improvement Association. His were among the twenty-six pairs of eyes that gazed down from that wall. This basement was the place where I had been interviewed by the pastoral search committee. You can imagine how I felt during that interview to be seated facing the photos of the giants who had piloted this great church before me.

As any newcomer to such an arena would, I searched deeply in my own soul and asked, "Lord what will you have me to do?" "What talents do I bring to the table?" and a hundred other similar questions. The question that most intrigued me concerned the directions in which my predecessors had attempted to take the church. Institutions are products of leadership. I often wondered about their leadership strengths and weaknesses, their visions for the church, etc. I desperately wanted insight to these questions, because I now stand on the shoulders of these giants. Their tenures here, their sojourns here, directly impact my own sojourn upon these hallowed grounds.

Voices from the Dexter Pulpit evolved from an emerging desire I felt to invite the six pastors of Dexter since 1960 to participate in some meaningful project together. Rarely does one have an opportunity to glean insight from such a distinguished host of predecessors. All these men gave positive leadership and made an impact upon Dexter and then moved on to do other things in life as God called them.

During their tenure at Dexter they performed the rites of baptism, marriage, and burial for their parishioners. They kept the congregation going as they sought God's direction. It was my hope that such a project would add to the ongoing legacy of the church, which is often shrouded in mystery. I felt that bringing the six living pastors of Dexter together would result in wholesome dialogue about the church and its direction today and provide a strong rallying point for the congregation.

Looking for some occasion in which to build a point of dialogue with my predecessors, I had the idea to invite them to contribute a sermon, either one they had delivered while here at Dexter, or one they would like to address today to the present Dexter congregation. Thus was born the idea of "Voices from the Dexter Pulpit," not as a history of the Dexter Avenue Baptist Church, but rather a collection of sermonic essays from its past pastors.

MY GREATEST thanks must go to my fellow contributors of the sermons. Such an undertaking would not have been possible without their prompt response to the request and without the wisdom and eloquence of their words.

I am deeply indebted to Randall Williams and Suzanne LaRosa of NewSouth Books, who immediately saw the possibilities for a work of this nature. It has been through their assistance that this has become a reality. I also wish to express profound thanks to Ben Beard, Faithe Hurst, Mildred Wakefield, Vanessa Teacher, and Wendy Mann of the NewSouth staff for their continued faith and confidence in me that I would get it done, and for their work in the trenches of book publishing. Albeit there were many hurdles to cross, I was determined not to let them down.

While I have now started to express acknowledgments, I cannot forget my wife, Pat, who over the years has pushed me to write. Not a month has gone by over the last ten years that Pat has not mentioned that I should be writing. When I would desperately seek God's purpose for my life, Pat would remind me that writing ought be included in my plans. I am also indebted to Pat for assisting with the typing. I cannot forget our children, Tanerica and Jonathan, who supported me through this effort and allowed Daddy the quality time to get the work done, often sacrificing their time with me to ensure that I completed the project.

I also wish to express a profound thanks to the deacons, trustees, and members of the Dexter Avenue King Memorial Baptist Church, who have given me broad latitude to explore the complete dimensions of my calling here at Dexter. This book was completed during the summer of 2000, an extremely busy period for me at Dexter. I spent May and June traveling to several cities on a project, "The Revitalization of Historical African-American Churches," funded by the Louisville Institute, a program of the Lilly Endowment. I began a series of bi-monthly meetings (also sponsored by Lilly Endowment and the Louisville Institute) with a group of twelve clergy from across the country with the expressed purpose being to explore dimensions of pastoral and congregational life. This summer also marked the kick-off of some major internal ministry plans here at the church.

I am furthermore, indebted to a number of Dexterites who encouraged me. Mrs. Margaret Beverly first encouraged me to keep a journal shortly upon my arrival here at Dexter. Needless to say, I have fallen short of this duty, but as always, promise to get with it. Many others in the wings of church life have wished me well both with their prayers and with their kind words of encouragement. For this I am thankful!

Deacon Virginia Gary proved to be a gem! She would laboriously read through nearly every word, phrase, sentence, paragraph and page of the project and check it for grammar and spelling. Deacon Gary serves as the church's librarian and we here at Dexter are indebted to her for her services.

I also wish to express a hearty thanks to the various persons to whom I would occasionally farm out pieces of the project for their comments: namely, senior deacon Robert Nesbitt, Sr., Thomas McPherson, Frenetter Conway, Connie Harper, and Gene Crum.

This list would not be complete if I did not say thanks to my mother and father, Dr. Willie and Mamie Muse. Mom and Dad have stood behind me and provided great support in the many endeavors I have undertaken. I can still remember Mother and I walking down Peachtree Street in Atlanta soon after I had accepted work with the Home Mission Board of the Southern Baptist Convention. She admonished me, "You be sure to give those for whom you labor an honest day's work for an honest day's pay." This philosophy carries over with me even until this day!

I want to thank Dr. Leon Howard Sullivan, who has touched my life in more ways than I can yet fully fathom. I have looked to Dr. Sullivan many times as the going got tough on this project and others. He has become a model for my life and a testimony as to what can be done if one keeps a steady head and stays the course and allows God to use him as an instrument. Dr. Sullivan has been a silent mentor for me. He shall be greatly missed.

I would like to add a special thanks to the staff of Internation Foundation for Education and Self-Help for there assistance in getting the Foreword completed following Dr. Sullivan's death. Dr. C. T. Wright and Mrs. Pearleana Jackson were most helpful in this endeavor.

Special thanks to Philip Cusic and Hayward Horton, two friends who have encouraged me to write over the years and have been sounding boards for ideas and concepts. He who has friends truly has a more precious treasure than gold and silver.

I wish to express gratitude to both the families of Vernon Johns and Martin Luther King, Jr., for granting permission to use the enclosed sermons.

Finally, special thanks to Andrea Johnson, who assisted with the typing of the project, and to Cora Thomas, for helping me keep track of the contributors and for keeping me informed of the publishers' concerns.

Thanks to God, for helping me keep my sanity through it all and giving me the strength to journey on.

It is not the critic who counts, not the man who points out how the strong man stumbled or where the doer of the deeds could have done them better. The credit belongs to the man who is actually in the arena: whose face is marred by dust and sweat and blood; who strives valiantly; who errs and comes up short again and again; who knows the great enthusiasms, the great devotions and spends himself in a worthy cause; who, at the best, knows the triumph of high achievement; and who, at the worst, if he fails, at least fails daring greatly, so that his place shall never be with those cold and timid souls who know neither victory nor defeat.

—JOHN F. KENNEDY

Introduction

Millions of pilgrims make their way to Montgomery, Alabama, each year to visit the historical sites of a most unusual city. Montgomery has been rightfully dubbed the birthplace of both Civil War and Civil Rights. It is almost miraculous that two of the nation's pivotal events took place within a few blocks of each other. Who could have predicted in 1830, when slaves were being sold like horseflesh at the present site of the majestic fountain in Montgomery's Court Square, that in less than fifty years freed slaves would begin building their own church on broad Dexter Avenue? Who could have imagined the separation of one city block and one century between the Alabama State Capitol, where Jefferson Davis pronounced the creation of a new nation dedicated to slavery, and the Dexter Avenue Baptist Church, where both Dr. Vernon Johns and Dr. Martin Luther King, Jr., led their people away from the legacy of slavery?

Confronted with the stark reality that here stands a Negro institution of protest at the base of the citadel of the Southern white power structure, one is immediately presented with the humor of God. This is irony at its best!

The Dexter church property was purchased on January 30, 1879, for two hundred and seventy dollars. (The congregation itself is two years older, having begun meeting in 1877 in a structure that was, in a remarkable irony, a crude pen previously used by a slave trader to hold his human merchandise.) Many people ask how African Americans were able to acquire such prime property in Montgomery's central business district during the time period right after the war? The only logical explanation is that the church's trustees purchased the property during the narrow window of Union Army occupation and the progressive social policies of Reconstruction. That window quickly closed beginning in the 1880s as Southern whites regained control and began fashioning the Jim Crow laws that would define life in the South for almost a century. The 1954 *Brown v. Board of Education* decision by the U.S. Supreme Court was the first major victory toward the establishment of equality for Negroes in America since Reconstruction ended in 1878. So the acquisition of the Dexter church property was a matter of timing and Divine Providence.

Dexter and similar churches played an essential role in the development of the African American community. These churches came into existence as a response to the mandate of Christ through a creative synthesis, a unique blend of African culture and American religion fashioned both out of the slave quarters of the South and communities of free urban blacks in the North. Constituents of this powerful new institution were barred from participation in white churches. It is not an exaggeration to state that during this period the black church was the only institution wholly owned by African Americans.

In *The Souls of Black Folk*, W. E. B. Dubois states, "the Negro church antedates the black family." During slavery,

African American familial relations were often deliberately disregarded—either as punishment for disobedience or simply for the economic gain of the slave master—for the sake of business transactions. It was the church that helped these disfranchised families to pick up the broken pieces and move toward spiritual and emotional wholeness. The church provided moral stability and development of skills and education for a recently freed class of people; thus the African American church became both an ethics and morality center as well as an educational institutional. It was out of such a rich tradition that the Dexter Avenue Baptist Church rose.

Dubois wrote that three things distinguish the African American church: the preacher, the music, and the frenzy. Well, maybe not in all cases. The Dexter congregation has always prided itself as being somewhat reserved in its worship style. But the black preacher is indeed a unique creation on American soil! Some have attempted to trace his origins to that of the old medicine man of African tribes, and other scholars have alluded to the similarities between the preacher and the tribal chief as a unique blend of personalities. Still others hold that the black preacher arose out of an entirely unique set of circumstances peculiar to America and nurtured by the oppressive conditions that African Americans found themselves in this country. The black preacher in America, armed with a powerful conviction that God was on the side of the oppressed, began to create a redemptive environment for those shackled in a distorted mindset of their worth and dignity in society.

During Dexter's 125-year history it has enjoyed outstanding pastoral leadership. Its notable pastors include Charles O. Booth, R. T. Pollard, Robert Judkins, W. H. McAlpine, W. W. Colley, Ralph Riley, Vernon Johns, and Martin Luther King,

Jr. The archives of our church make it clear that our pastors served both church and community with distinction, making an impact within both spheres, during all the decades since Dexter's founding. For most of those decades, the extent of black participation in the worlds of business, government, and other "official" life was severely circumscribed by the law and custom of Jim Crow segregation. With rare exception, African Americans could not hold office, vote, travel without restriction, be considered for most jobs, obtain professional educations, or any of a hundred other soul-crippling limitations. Between the end of Reconstruction and the 1954 Supreme Court decision in *Brown v. Board of Education*, there were many disappointments and few victories in the history of black America.

But following World War II, in which African Americans bled and died for democracy abroad while being painfully aware they did not enjoy democracy at home, attitudes and conditions began to change. In Montgomery, young veteran members of Dexter Avenue Baptist Church were among those who had a new intensity in their desire to achieve human and civil rights. It must have been Divine Providence again that sent Dr. Vernon Johns and Dr. Martin Luther King, Jr., as pastors to Dexter in this critical period at the outset of the 20th century civil rights movement in the United States.

Johns's role is not as well-known as that of King, but both were the right men in the right place at the right time. In light of the Johns–King era, persons from around the world have come to view Dexter as a major religious icon, indeed as a very embodiment of liberation. Dexter has come to be recognized as one of the African American pillar institutions, which has nurtured the spirit of freedom among a people who fought bravely and valiantly against socioeconomic disparity. Dexter has become a symbol of hope to millions around the world.

In the corporate history and culture of any institution there are those who have been entrusted with the ongoing struggle of piloting the organization. These are the persons who must examine the organization from its many facets and bring focus to the issues of the current day and point the organization into some positive direction. At Dexter, these leaders are the pastors whom God has chosen to place within the life of this great church for the timeframe in which they served. Upon their shoulders has rested the heavy burden of lifting the institution that it might be an even brighter beacon in yet another dark hour.

As I explained in the preface, my aim with *Voices from the Dexter Pulpit* was to bring together six of the pastors who have filled the Dexter pulpit since Dr. King resigned in 1960. I asked each of my predecessors to contribute a sermon which either challenged the congregation concerning its moral obligation to lead in the quest for justice and equality, or which attempted to aid the church in capturing a vision. I then decided that it would be a pleasure for readers as well as enlightening to include one sermon each from Johns and King, and having made that addition, I decided to add a brief essay about the sociological and theological underpinnings of the Johns–King era.

That essay precedes the sermons, and then the sermons are arranged in the chronological order in which the pastors served, from Johns to myself.

The pastors and their years of service are:

Vernon Johns, 1947–1952*
Martin Luther King, Jr., 1954–1960
Herbert Eaton, 1960–1965
G. Murray Branch, 1966–1972
Robert Dickerson, 1972–1977
G. Murray Branch, 1977–1989
Boykin Sanders, 1990–1991
Richard Wills, 1992–1995

And in 1996, I was called to be the twenty-seventh pastor of the Dexter Avenue King Memorial Baptist Church family.

It is my sincere hope that you will enjoy the sermonic essays which appear in this volume. I trust that as you read the sermons on the following pages that you will catch a glimpse of the answer to the arresting question, "What is it like to stand in that pulpit?" It can be only a glimpse, of course, for I know from personal experience that one can never grasp the complete essence of the awesome weight of that task and that responsibility without having had to seek God's will and purpose for the church as its leader. But a sermon suggests a struggle to provide spiritual uplift, direction, and information through the prophetic medium of the preached Word. It is my hope that these collected sermons will shed light on the challenge and struggle each man faced as they stepped into one of the most historic pulpits in the world.

---

*Dexter was without a full-time pastor for the two-year period between Johns and King.

I

A Socio-Theological Analysis of the Johns-King Era

Michael Thurman

Vernon Johns and Martin Luther King, Jr., are among the very best products of the African American church. They are the embodiments of liberation theology and are models of African American pastor, theologian, and activist for all seasons. These two men will be the topic of theological debate for decades to come, as new generations of African Americans search for timely solutions to combat the problems of injustice in American society and as this injustice takes on a more global face as we move into the widening arena of multiculturalism. Even the broader umbrella of evangelical Christendom has found a powerful model of social activism within the African American church, as the white evangelical church has come to the forefront of policy shaping in the venue of right-wing Christianity and the conservative, fundamentalist resurgence.

It is remarkable that these two men should have landed in the same pulpit within a span of two years. Johns served Dexter from 1947 until 1952 and King from 1954 until 1960. Both had unique styles, though there were probably more similarities than differences. Once one gets past the superficial differences of personal style—Vernon Johns was brash, outspoken and eccentric, while Martin King was refined and poised—then one can begin to focus on the things they had in common.

First and foremost, both had a solid commitment to reshape the society in which they lived for justice and equality for all persons. Their methods were different. Johns was a one-man protest movement, executed through a series of sporadic, bombastic tactics, while King built coalitions and mobilized masses of people and attacked the system through well-planned assaults. Both put their lives on the line to validate their convictions. Their quests for freedom and justice were not mundane feelings ignited from time to time by some quaint incidents, but rather were at the core of their beings. It was this basic drive that propelled them to protest the unjust laws and customs that had become ingrained into American culture. Johns and King *had* to stand up for human rights because they were convinced that doing so was the "will of the Creator."

In my own thinking on the socio-theological implications of their ministries, I borrow heavily from a prominent Jewish theologian, the late Abraham Heschel, former professor of Old Testament at Jewish Theological Seminary. I admire Heschel's work, which I became acquainted with when his book, *The Prophet,* was used as a textbook for a class I taught at the Montgomery Bible Institute. I also admire Heschel's personal convictions because he felt compelled to march across the Edmund Pettus Bridge in Selma, Alabama, in 1965. Heschel said in reference to his involvement in the Selma March that "I prayed with my feet."

Prophet is an accurate term to describe Vernon Johns and Martin King. They were modern day prophets with a mission similar to that of the more familiar Old Testament prophets. We are most comfortable with prophets within the context of Biblical theology and within the geographical region of Palestine. However, we balk at the notion that God continues to make known his will to mankind through spokespersons who appear on the scene at various times. In my own understanding of the will of God, I firmly believe that Vernon Johns was to Martin King what John the Baptist was to Jesus—a type of forerunner with a divine mission and purpose to set the stage for justice and equality.

Heschel, in writing on "What manner of man is the prophet?", identifies seventeen attributes which define the persona of the prophet. We will rely upon a few of Heschel's attributes to describe the ministries of Vernon Johns and Martin King.

First, the prophet has a keen sensitivity to evil. Whereas most of us have been acculturated to be tolerant, the prophet is greatly pained by evil. Vernon Johns and Martin King were such persons. While the masses of African Americans and whites alike have a "don't rock the boat" approach to life even when conditions are unfair and unjust, as was the case with segregation laws, the prophet of God feels a tremendous burden to address the injustice as if the injustice were perpetrated upon his own person. This is why Johns felt morally obligated to address the unjustified murder of an unarmed black man by Montgomery police, and mounted the Dexter pulpit and preached a sermon entitled, "It is Safe to Murder Negroes." This also explains why Dr. King was willing to endure numerous threats upon his life and even the lives of his family.

A second major attribute of the prophet is the prophet's conviction that God is infinitely concerned about the affairs of man. Heschel terms this the "importance of trivialities." A major proposition of liberation theology is that God is on the side of the oppressed. King and Johns both believed that God would one day vindicate the righteous, but that man must take an active role in bringing about that change. One stanza of "We Shall Overcome," the theme song of the civil rights movement, is, "God is on our side! God is on our side! God is on our side, today! O, deep in my heart, I do believe that God is on our side, today!" Both men were thoroughly convinced that God cared about the plight of the Negro in America and was deeply concerned about him as a human being and was also concerned about his socioeconomic well-being. Johns and King firmly believed that God would bring about justice and the time for this supra-correction of history was long overdue.

Within the unique Dexter ministries of Vernon Johns and Martin Luther King, Jr., one gets a sense that a prophet possesses qualities that Heschel regards as "luminous and explosive." Heschel says:

> Authentic utterances derives from a moment of identification of a people and a word; its significance depends upon the urgency and magnitude of its theme. The prophet's theme is the very life of a whole people . . . his life and soul are at stake in what he says and in what is going to happen to what he says . . . Prophetic utterances are rarely cryptic, suspended between God and man; it is urging, alarming, forcing onward, as if the words gushed forth from the heart of God, seeking entrance into the heart and mind of man.

King and Johns both had a powerful theme that would be broadcast across America in a way that would inspire literally thousands of clergy. Vernon Johns's message would not be appreciated until much later—by both his Dexter parishioners and a much larger audience of church leaders who would come to look back to Johns as a model of ministry. (Two prominent church leaders who were touched by the message of Vernon Johns are Leon Sullivan and Wyatt T. Walker.) The constant theme of the ministries of Vernon Johns and Martin Luther King, Jr., was to eliminate segregation and to build a strong society in which all persons irrespective of race, class, or creed could fully participate. They trumpeted this message from the Dexter pulpit and wherever they journeyed, for it was a part of their identity. They were thoroughly convinced that this message of equality and justice had its genesis in the very heart of God.

Another major attribute of the prophet, according to Heschel, involved the prophet's appeal to the highest good. The prophet would lift his voice and pronounce doom and despair for individuals and nations alike, but he would always appeal to the highest good innate within every man. Martin King even reminded us to seek the highest good within our enemy. As the best of man's intentions must necessarily fall short of the glory of God, even man's most noble accomplishment would amount to nothing within the abodes of glory. So the prophet would point his constituents to the highest standard of example possible—he would attempt to reveal God Himself. As King and Johns served the Dexter Church family and the broader Montgomery community, they made a conscious effort to appeal to the highest standard of ethical behavior as exemplified in God Almighty, and they in essence became mouthpieces for Him and allowed themselves to be consumed by his love, justice, compassion, and anger.

The prophet is often a step ahead of the rest of society. He/ she moves to the beat of a different drummer, or perhaps they hear the same drumbeat but they hear it before the masses do. Heschel suggests that within the attributes of the prophet one finds that the prophet is "one octave too high." We find especially in the eccentric personality of Vernon Johns that he indeed was ahead of his time as he challenged African Americans to become more assertive about business ownership and economic development opportunities. Johns used his personal funds along with support from a few early "venture capitalists" (mostly working-class persons and teachers) to establish a market where produce and other food items were sold. When Johns resorted to marketing his produce on the corner of Dexter Avenue and Decatur Street, right in front of the church, this was too much for some of the bourgeoisie membership of Dexter. Similar incidents brought about his dismissal from the church. When King led the Montgomery Bus Boycott in 1955-56 and gradually became involved in subsequent public demonstrations, his broader ministry also inevitably led to some attempts to silence the prophet from within the very ranks of those whose freedom he sought to secure. We must remember that the prophet's role is not to make us feel good but is instead to stir us to action and thereby to effect change.

Still another attribute of the prophet helps to shed light on the Johns–King era at Dexter. Heschel indicates that the prophet is an iconoclast, one who challenges institutions and ideals which are the very fabric of society. Like the Old Testament prophets, Johns and King challenged the very framework of segregation, Johns in the police brutality case and King in the Montgomery Bus Boycott. Johns had also staged, several years before the Rosa Parks incident, a one-man protest against segregated public transportation. These are merely examples of Johns's and King's unwavering commitment to justice and equality. As iconoclasts they focused their attention and energies on the evils of the system and not necessarily the individuals who ran the system, for those persons were themselves simply a product of a misguided culture.

Interestingly, King found and employed one of the most effective weapons for dealing with a society whose laws promoted injustice and inequality. This was the weapon of passive resistance and nonviolence. Through mass public demonstrations combined with nonviolence and love, and perhaps through the power of the media, King was able to show the contrast between the ideals of democracy and the realities of segregation in America. Gradually public awareness increased and public anger rose, which led to changes in attitudes and to support for changes in the courts and legislatures. But it all began with the attack on the failure of American democracy to deliver a fair and just society for all.

Final attributes to examine are austerity and compassion. Heschel suggests that the prophet has a unique balance of sternness and compassion. The prophet applies the necessary social pressure and force needed to get God's message over, but even in his sternness there is moral compassion. One can sense this striving for balance in Dr. King's "I have a Dream" speech, which clearly points to the shortcomings of American democracy but just as clearly points to the ideal that these shortcomings will be rectified. There was compassion even behind King's austerity. His quest was not unlike that of any father for the world within which his children lived to become a better place.

In retrospect, Vernon Johns and Martin Luther King, Jr., were modern prophets who marched to the steady beat of a

"Moral Drum Major." Johns and King were trumpeters who played a constant note on the musical scale of justice. In the wake of this band having played a half century ago, the Moral Drum Major continues to lead the band and other trumpeters continue to sound the notes on the brass horns of social reform today. Countless legions of young men and women have been inspired by the works and words of King and Johns. And just as there were some strong trumpeters in Montgomery, others across the nation were sounding similar notes; they did not enjoy the renown of Johns and King, yet nevertheless they were effective in their own rights and within their own contexts. The period of the fifties and sixties marked one of the finest hours for the African American church. This is not to say that the African American church has seen its best days, for the African American church remains the only institution equipped to combat the vast social ills within our communities. Through innovative means our churches will be called upon again and again to apply the healing balm in order to soothe the pain of its constituents as we face new challenges in the years to come.

Vernon Johns and Martin King taught us how to fight in the old tradition of Nat Turner, Richard Allen, George Liele, and other pivotal African American religious leaders. As we engage in the same battle on a new frontier, the issues of environmental racism, health (including AIDS, heart disease, diabetes, etc.), education, housing, corporate glass ceilings, business ownership, and the list goes on, the African American church will be called upon to provide leadership for the nameless and the faceless. But we must seek new methods to broaden the struggle to include other victims of the failure of American democracy, and we must bring them to the table of brotherhood and flesh out an agenda that will provide for the uplift of all people. The African American church must discover ways in which it can incorporate the poor and disfranchised of all groups and build effective coalitions. There is a serious need to collaborate on community-based projects, projects that would be too large for any one church, as we seek to combine our energies for a common cause. This would multiply our efforts and effectiveness exponentially.

2

Transfigured Moments

Vernon Johns

Then answered Peter, and said unto Jesus, Lord, it is
good for us to be here: if thou wilt, let us
make here three tabernacles; one for thee, and one
for Moses, and one for Elijah.

Matthew 17:4

Peter, James, and John, who had already gone with the Master to the death bed in the house of Jairus, and would very soon come closer to his agony in Gethsemane than the other disciples, were now with him in "a place apart," somewhere on the slopes of Hermon. Strange things were happening there: things difficult for people to believe until they have felt the unfathomed mystery of life, and learned that "there are more things in heaven and earth than we have dreamed in our philosophy." As the Divine man prayed that night, on the snow-capped mountain, with the weight of humanity's sin and humanity's hope upon his heart, his disciples beheld his body suddenly overcast with an unfamiliar luster. His pure soul had overflowed and clothed his figure with a wonderful radiance. His face shone as the sun, and Moses and

Elijah, venerable pioneers of law and prophecy, had come through the intervening mystery which separates the living from the dead, and were talking with Jesus, within sight and hearing of the disciples. Then a voice broke forth from the luminous cloud: "This is my beloved son: hear ye him!"

Anyone acquainted with Simon Peter will not be surprised if he speaks now. He is the type of man who can be depended on to say what others must need think and feel, but dare not utter. He was a valuable man to Jesus: a rock foundation man, for this very reason he revealed his thoughts and made it possible for Jesus to give them direction.

Bishop McConnell says that Peter asked many foolish questions, but those questions brought from Jesus very wise answers. It would be difficult for us to sojourn with Simon and dodge sensitive questions, covering up grave issues that so nearly concern us, and trying to hide them from ourselves as though they did not exist. The blundering genius for expression, which was the virtue of Simon Peter, would save us from the folly of applying ostrich wisdom to vital problems. If we had the courage to talk frankly concerning our problems, there would be less occasion to fight about them. In grave moral and social situations where the spokesmen of Jesus, so-called, keep dependably mute, Simon Peter would certainly have something to say or at least ask some embarrassing questions. Peter was a true disciple of the one who came to earth "That thoughts out of many hearts might be revealed."

So on the Mount of Transfiguration, while experiencing was rife, James reflected deeply, John thrilled with awe, and Peter spoke! Peter felt the tides running high in his soul; and he said so: "Lord it is good to be here." When Peter has a weighty idea or a generous impulse, it is likely to get expression. No

This enlargement from an old newspaper clipping is the only photo of Vernon Johns that the Dexter Church possesses. Johns (1892–1965) was born in Virginia and received his early education at Boyton Institute. He graduated from Virginia Theological Seminary (A.B., 1915) and Oberlin College Graduate School of Theology (B.D., 1918). Ordained to the ministry in 1918, he pastored numerous churches before landing at Dexter in 1947, where he remained until 1952.

matter what celebrities are present, no matter how delicate the situation, no mater if he breaks down short of the goal which he sets for himself; at least his Master may count on him to give honest expression to the best that he knows and feels. This is the man whom Jesus commissions to feed his sheep and lambs.

This is the foundation man, on whose God-inspired utterance the Kingdom will be built against which the gates of hell shall not prevail. One of the biographers of Jesus felt it necessary to apologize for Peter's speech during the Transfiguration. "He knew not what to say, for he was so afraid." There are always disciples, more cautious but less valuable than Peter, who guard their words very zealously in tense situations, and for fear they may say something indiscreet will almost certainly be silent. They talk most when there is but little need to say anything, and the topic of their conversation is not likely to be material which will spread fire in the earth or set a father against his son, or make a man's enemies those of his own household. There are things "that Babbitt will not talk about." No apology was really needed for what Peter said. Who can doubt that it was good to be there, high upon Hermon, in those Transfigured Moments! The experience was so rich and lasting that it went to record, many years later, in three of the Gospels and one New Testament epistle: and the glory which shone that night, in "a mountain place apart," lingers after two thousand years on every continent and over every sea.

It is good to be the possessor of some mountain-top experience. Not to know life on the heights is to suffer an impoverishing incompleteness. To be sure, there is better opportunity for practical pursuits in the valley regions, and life is easier and safer there; but views are possible from the mountain top which are not to be had in the vale. A missionary in the Balkans once took a small boy, who lived at the base of a mountain, on a journey up its side. When they gained the summit, the little climber looked this way and that, and then said with astonishment: "My! What a wonderful world. I never dreamed it was large." Horizons broaden when we stand on the heights.

There is always the danger that we will make of life too much of a dead-level existence; that we will make a slavish following of the water courses, a monotonous tread of beaten paths, a matter of absorbing, spiritless, deadening routine. There is the danger that we will drop our lives into the passing current to be kept steadily going, we hardly know where or why. Crowded in the throngs that traverse the common ways, we proceed through life with much motion and little vision. The late President Wilson, in a wonderful essay, speaks of the man who allows his duties to rise about him like a flood.

Such a man goes on through the years "swimming with sturdy stroke, his eyes level with the surface, never seeing any clouds or any passing ships." We can pay such regular tribute to motion that all valid sense of direction is lost; so that all our hurrying activities may prove but the rush to ruin. In view of this, it is good for us, occasionally at least, to clamber up from the levels of our set habits of thought, our artificial actions and our settled prejudices, to some loftier plane which affords a more commanding view than we have from the crowded thoroughfares, the low familiar ways. From some mountain eminence let us have occasionally a quiet look upon life, to reflect what it means and whither it is carrying us.

The luminaries of humanity were familiar with elevated ground. Moses, Elijah, Mohammad, and Jesus all had mountain traditions. It is said by a well-known Old Testament interpreter that the religious history of the Hebrew people is inseparable from the topography of their country. The mountains round about Jerusalem are tied up with the vision of God and the vision of life, which Israel gave to mankind.

It is good to be present when the ordinary is transformed, when the dull plain garments of a peasant become shining white, and the obscure "Mountain place, apart" comes into the gaze of centuries. It is good to see the commonplace illumined and the glory of the common people revealed. On the Mount of Transfiguration there is no representative of wealth, social rank, or official position. The place could boast in the way of population only four poor men, members of a despised race, and of the remnant of a subjected and broken nation. But it is here, instead of Jerusalem or Rome, that the voice of God is heard. It is here, instead of Mount Moriah, where the mighty temple stands, that the cloud of glory hovers. Out there where a carpenter and three fishermen kept vigil with the promise of a new day, God is a living Reality and life is charged with meaning and radiance. Out there in a deserted place, the meek and lowly are enhaloed.

There is no recounting the instances where the things that are excellent have blossomed in unexpected places. "He giveth power to the faint; and to them that have no might He increaseth strength." A man who is not a prophet, neither a prophet's son, is called by the Lord from following the sheep to prophesy to the House of Israel. In the heyday of Egyptian civilization, God visits the wilderness of Midian and commissions a shepherd for the most significant work of the age:

> In the fifteenth year of the reign of Tiberius Caesar,
> Pontius Pilate being governor of Judea, and Herod tetrarch of
> Galilee, and his brother Philip tetrarch of Iturea and the

region of Trachonitis, and Lysanias the tetrarch of Abilene; in
the high priesthood of Annas and Caiphas, the word of the
Lord came to John the son of Zacharias, in the wilderness.

"Who is this man that is answering Douglas in your State?"
wrote a prominent statesman of the East, to the editor of a
Chicago paper, concerning the unheralded Lincoln. "Do you
realize that his knowledge of the most important question
before the American people is complete and profound; that his
logic is unanswerable and his style inimitable?" It is the illumi-
nation of the commonplace, the transfiguring of the ordinary,
the glistening radiance of a peasant's seamless robe!

There are two ways in which this transfiguring of the
ordinary is specially needed. The lowly ones of Earth need to
experience this transformation. The great majority of our lives
must be lived apart from any elaborate or jeweled settings; we
must plod along without any spectacular achievements. We
ordinary people, then, must learn how to set the scraggly bushes
of the wilderness ablaze with glory and make the paths that we
tread, under the pressure of duty, like Holy Ground! In the
humblest routine, we must discover our task as a part of the
transforming enterprise of the Heavenly Father. The laborer
that toils on a country road must know himself as the builder of
a highway to a Christian civilization. The cobbler may be a
mere cobbler, or he may transform his occupation and be a
Foundation Man in the Kingdom of Christ. Make tents if we
must, but we will illumine the old task with a radiant new heart,
and, with our tent-making, make a shining new earth. If toil be
confined to the same old fields, keep a land of promise shining
in the distance and call down angels to sing until the drab turns
golden. "My garden is very small," said an old German, "but it

is wondrous high." Let us light up the commonplace and make the ordinary radiant. Let us make seamless peasant garments shine like the sun.

Again, those who think themselves the favored ones of Earth need a transforming vision of life among the lowly. There is no warrant in the theory and practice of Jesus for dull and frigid doctrines of "lesser breeds within the law." If the life of Jesus means anything, it means implicit faith in the universal capacity of man for the highest character and worth. To this end, the doors of the kingdom of the best are thrown open to all the points of the compass that men may "come from the North and the South, the East and the West to sit down with Abraham and Isaac, in the Kingdom of God." A low theory, a despicable view of a given group must usually be thrown ahead like a barrage before we can follow with the outrage and mistreatment of that group. We make them Hydra-headed in theory so that we may be inhuman in our practice toward them. The validity for such judgment crops out unaware at times, as when masters avow their slaves' inability to learn and at the same time penalize them if caught with a book. Humanity that has climbed to places of social and economic authority must learn how to trace the rainbow tint over the life of the lowly, and to interpret the swelling and ferment at the bottom of society as a healthy and beautiful essay of one's fellow men in the direction of fuller life. It is a heart strangely unChristlike that cannot thrill with joy when the least of men begin to pull in the direction of the stars.

It is good to be in the presence of persons who can kindle us for fine, heroic living.

The population on the Mount of Transfiguration was very small, but it was tremendously significant. Jesus, Moses, and

Elijah! In the presence of personality like this, men can kindle their torches and go forth in life as bearers of light and heat. Humanity needs the contagion of lofty spirits. Humanity needs contact with persons who are aglow with the good life. All too frequently our righteousness is sufficiently meager to go to waste: it is not vital enough to communicate itself. Mr. Roosevelt's criticism of his progressive party was that it meant well, but meant it feebly. That is often the trouble with our righteousness. It lacks intensity. It does not make itself felt. We are trying to grind great mills with a quart of water; we would set great masses of cold and slimy material aglow with a wet match. We have our hands full of halfway measures. We scrap a part of our navies. We enthrone Justice in places where there is no serious objection to it. We practice brotherhood within carefully restricted areas. We forgive other people's enemies. We carry a Bible but not a cross. Instead of the Second Mile, we go a few yards of the first and then wonder that Christian goals are not realized. "O fools and slow of heart to believe all that the prophets have spoken!" When we lift ourselves, at least from the ruin and entanglements of our diluted and piecemeal righteousness, it will be under the leadership of persons for whom righteousness was a consuming and holy fire, instead of a mere lukewarm and foggy something. It is such leadership, such righteous dynamics as this that we find in the presence of Jesus and Moses and Elijah. "We beheld his glory, glory as of the only begotten of the Father, full of grace and truth. And of his fullness we have all received." You can kindle at a flame like that! It is the full receptacle that overflows, spreading its content to neighboring borders. It is a flame vital enough not to be extinguished by a slight jostle at which men can kindle. "I have come to set a fire in the earth."

We need power for renunciation. In the service of social progress, justice, and brotherhood there are views and possessions of which one must have power to let go. Nothing short of power will work the transformation. But we are apt to hang on to our self-love, our vantage points, our place with the strong, our purpose of self-advancement. And we get no strength for the demands laid upon us from the weaklings on our level. But here on the mountain top is personality in which the power of renunciation rises to white heat!

> By faith, Moses when he was come to years, refused to be called the son of Pharaoh's daughter, choosing rather to suffer affliction with the people of God than to enjoy the pleasures of sin for a season; esteeming the reproach of Christ greater riches than the treasure of Egypt.

When this ancient Hero exchanged a princely existence at court for exile in Midian, and defied the oppressor in the interest of the oppressed, he lighted a flame at which humanity through thousands of years has kindled power for heroic renunciation. It is good to sit in the presence of Moses if one is to live the life of heroic self-denial.

And there is a power on the Mount of Transfiguration, which kindles tongues and sends forth in evil times for the service of justice. Ahab the king has lifted his bloody hand against a weak subject. He has killed Naboth and taken his patch of land to fill out a nook in one of the royal estates. It is a dastardly act, but Naboth is weak and Ahab mighty, so the voices of justice are not heard. Tyranny broods restfully over the face of the nation. Murder and robbery issue from the very seat of law; and all is well. Thank God, here comes a loud, clear note of discord in the evil harmony! Ahab has gone down to his ill-gotten vineyard and Elijah meets him there. No one can stand with Elijah in that garden without feeling the thrill of manhood: it is a fine place to kindle holy courage. Mighty is Ahab in Israel, but mighty also is Elijah in the service of truth. The Tisbite, in his camel's hair, rubs against the purple of a king mighty in war and peace. He does not wait for royal permission. One listening to that conversation, without seeing the participants, would have mistaken peasant for king and king for peasant.

> "Hast thou killed and also taken possession? Hast thou found me, O mine enemy?" And Elijah answered, "I have found thee; and thus saith the Lord in the spot where dogs licked the blood of Naboth, shall dogs lick thy blood."

The courage of Elijah is a glowing flame at which humanity has kindled power to shake the foundations of a thousand despotisms! And how Jesus could kindle people for courageous, loving, and lofty living! Here is Zacchaeus hovering at zero! His malady is not emotional, passionate weakness, but cold-blooded guile. He is a professional trader in the political misfortunes of his nation. His business is to sell the helplessness of his own race to the Roman overlord, and he has made the business pay. With Zacchaeus "business is business." The trouble with Zacchaeus is that he has never been shown a pattern of selfishness as large as his own selfishness. There have been little sputters of righteousness here and there, but nothing dramatic in that line. Zacchaeus feels some serious lack in connection with his own life and method, but he has never seen character the opposite of his own that was sufficiently large or radiant to be attractive. In the flaming proximity of Jesus the lost son of Israel finds himself. His frigidity thaws up: a new-found sense of justice and generosity blazes out: "Half of my goods I give to the poor, and if I have wronged any man by false accusation, I will restore unto him fourfold." At the flaming soul of Jesus, the frigid soul of Zacchaeus is set aglow.

Here is a woman who is a victim of a great primal emotion. Her name has dishonorable associations; her respect is buried deep beneath the ashes of excess. Each day finds her more shameless and deeper lost; each person passing throws a few more ashes upon the tiny spark of virtue left amid the embers. A lustful suggestion from this man, a contemptuous look from that woman, and the dim lingering vision of something wholesome and pure fades rapidly toward extinction. But Jesus comes along! In the atmosphere about him every slumbering impulse of love and purity begins to quicken. He discovers the faint spark in the ashes and embers and warms it to life. He is so pure himself that this poor woman, sunk to the depths, feels the contagion of his character pulling her toward the stars. A touch of shame mounts the throne in her cheek where a calloused indifference had sat: it turns to penitence and then to hope. "Can I become a worthy person in spite of all that is?" Her heart is asking the Master, and the Master, who understands the language of hearts and listens for it, answers:

> "Verily, I say unto you, wherever this gospel is preached in all the earth, your name and character shall attend it like the fragrance of precious ointment."

Again, the strength of a Personality, radiant with truth and love, had lifted a life from shame to sainthood.

Jesus kindled the consciousness of human brotherhood in the most self-conscious and provincial of all races. His character was so dramatically free from all class and national and racial hatred and prejudices that no follower could long mistake him. To mistake him would have been to cease following!

"There is no difference between Jew and Greek, barbarian, Scythian, bond or free, but all are one in Christ Jesus."

"I perceive that God is no respecter of persons, but in every nation they that fear God and work righteousness are acceptable with him."

"Out of one blood hath God created all nations to dwell upon the face of the earth."

This is the language of men who had kindled their lives at the feet of Jesus for the wise and noble adventure in human brotherhood.

It is good to be present when the great, distant peaks of history join hands to point the way of life: when seers, standing in different ages and places, one on Sinai, another on Carmel, and another on Olive, come together to speak to us out of the wisdom of the ages concerning the way and the meaning of life. All this is the privilege of those who frequent the heights! Up there we can read history with our eyes instead of our prejudices. Up there we do not hear the clamor of time-servers and self-servers. And as we look down from the heights, it is too far to descry the hue of faces or the peculiarity of skulls; all we can see is the forms of men, toiling or contending in the valleys – swayed by the same hopes and fears, the same joys and sorrows.

The whole creation groaning in travail and pain together and waiting for deliverance; one in need, one in destiny. "If drunk with sight of Power" we incline to boastings and vauntings, the seers on the heights say to us out of the wealth of the ages:

"Not by might; not by power; but by My Spirit, said the Lord." And they have wide inductions from the debris of many civilizations as warrant for the utterance. On the heights, too, there is hope for the world! Too often, history strikes us as a medley of blind and futile ramblings. "A tale told by an idiot amid great sound and fury, signifying nothing."

> "The drift of the Maker is dark."
> Into this Universe and why not knowing;
> Nor whence, like water willy-nilly flowing
> And out of it, like wind along the waste
> I go, I know not whither! Willy-nilly blowing.

But on the mountain-top, perspective is possible; above the confusion of the plains, the visitant beholds Moses in one age, Elijah in another, Jesus, Luther, and Lincoln, each in another; all joining hands across the Ages and moving humanity in the direction of that "one far off, divine event to which the whole creation moves."

It is good for us to be here.

3

A Knock at Midnight

MARTIN LUTHER KING, JR.

Which of you who has a friend will go to him at
midnight and say to him, "Friend, lend me three
loaves; for a friend of mine has arrived on a journey,
and I have nothing to set before him"?
Luke 11:5-6, RSV

Although this parable is concerned with the power of persistent prayer, it may also serve as a basis for our thought concerning many contemporary problems and the role of the church in grappling with them. It is midnight in the parable; it is also midnight in our world, and the darkness is so deep that we can hardly see which way to turn.

It is midnight within the social order. On the international horizon nations are engaged in a colossal and bitter contest for supremacy. Two world wars have been fought within a generation, and the clouds of another war are dangerously low. Man now has atomic and nuclear weapons that could within seconds completely destroy the major cities of the world. Yet the arms race continues and nuclear tests still explode in the atmosphere, with the grim prospect that the very air we breathe will be poisoned by radioactive fallout. Will these circumstances and weapons bring the annihilation of the human race?

When confronted by midnight in the social order we have in the past turned to science for help. And little wonder! On so many occasions science has saved us. When we were in the midnight of physical limitation and material inconvenience, science lifted us to the bright morning of physical and material comfort. When we were in the midnight of crippling ignorance and superstition, science brought us to the daybreak of the free and open mind. When we were in the midnight of dreaded plagues and diseases, science, through surgery, sanitation, and the wonder drugs, ushered in the bright day of physical health, thereby prolonging our lives and making for greater security and physical well-being. How naturally we turn to science in a day when the problems of the world are so ghastly and ominous.

But alas! Science cannot now rescue us, for even the scientist is lost in the terrible midnight of our age. Indeed science gave us the very instruments that threaten to bring universal suicide. So modern man faces a dreary and frightening midnight in the social order.

This midnight in man's external collective life is paralleled by midnight in his internal individual life. It is midnight within the psychological order. Everywhere paralyzing fears harrow people by day and haunt them by night. Deep clouds of anxiety and depression are suspended in our mental skies. More people are emotionally disturbed today than at any other time of human history. The psychopathic wards of our hospitals are crowded, and the most popular psychologists today are the psychoanalysts. Bestsellers in psychology are books such as

Martin Luther King, Jr. (1929–1968) was born and raised in Atlanta. He was a graduate of Morehouse College (B.A., 1948) and Boston University (Ph.D., 1954), and had also studied at Crozer Theological Seminary. Given what he did, it is remarkable to recall that Martin Luther King, Jr., was only 24 years old when he accepted his first pastorate at the church that now bears his name. A year later he stepped into the leadership of the Montgomery Bus Boycott, and within a few years was the most powerful voice for human and civil rights in the nation and perhaps the world. He was assassinated in 1968 but lives on in history and in the hearts of the masses.

Man Against Himself, The Neurotic Personality of Our Times, and *Modern Man in Search of a Soul.* Bestsellers in religion are such books as *Peace of Mind* and *Peace of Soul.* The popular clergyman preaches soothing sermons on "How to Be Happy" and "How to Relax." Some have been tempted to revise Jesus's command to read, "Go ye into all the world, keep your blood pressure down, and lo, I will make you a well-adjusted personality." All of this is indicative that it is midnight within the inner lives of men and women.

It is also midnight within the moral order. At midnight colors lose their distinctiveness and become a sullen shade of gray. Moral principles have lost their distinctiveness. For modern man, absolute right and absolute wrong are a matter of what the majority is doing. Right and wrong are relative to likes and dislikes and the customs of a particular community. We have unconsciously applied Einstein's theory of relativity, which properly described the physical universe, to the moral and ethical realm.

Midnight is the hour when men desperately seek to obey the eleventh commandment, "Thou shalt not get caught." According to the ethic of midnight, the cardinal sin is to be caught and the cardinal virtue is to get by. It is all right to lie, but one must lie with real finesse. It is all right to steal, if one is so dignified that, if caught, the charge becomes embezzlement, not robbery. It is permissible even to hate, if one so dresses his hating in the garments of love that hating appears to be loving. The Darwinian concept of the survival of the fittest has been substituted by a philosophy of the survival of the slickest. This mentality has brought a tragic breakdown of moral standards, and the midnight of moral degeneration deepens.

As in the parable, so in our world today, the deep darkness

of midnight is interrupted by the sound of a knock. On the door of the church millions of people knock. In this country the roll of church members is longer than ever before. More than one hundred and fifteen million people are at least paper members of some church or synagogue. This represents an increase of one hundred percent since 1929, although the population has increased by only thirty-one percent.

Visitors to Soviet Russia, whose official policy is atheistic, report that the churches in that nation not only are crowded, but that attendance continues to grow. Harrison Salisbury, in an article in *The New York Times*, states that Communist officials are disturbed that so many young people express a growing interest in the church and religion. After forty years of the most vigorous efforts to suppress religion, the hierarchy of the Communist party now faces the inescapable fact that millions of people are knocking on the door of the church.

This numerical growth should not be overemphasized. We must not be tempted to confuse spiritual power and large numbers. Jumboism, as someone has called it, is an utterly fallacious standard for measuring positive power. An increase in quantity does not automatically bring an increase in quality. A larger membership does not necessarily represent a correspondingly increased commitment to Christ. Almost always the creative, dedicated minority has made the world better. But although a numerical growth in church membership does not necessarily reflect a concomitant increase in ethical commitment, millions of people feel that the church provides an answer to the deep confusion that encompasses their lives. It is still the one familiar landmark where the weary traveler by midnight comes. It is the one house which stands where it has always stood, the house to which the man traveling at midnight either comes or refuses to come. Some decide not to come. But the many who come and knock are desperately seeking a little bread to tide them over.

The traveler asked for three loaves of bread. He wants the bread of faith. In a generation of so many colossal disappointments, men have lost faith in God, faith in man, and faith in the future. Many feel as did William Wilberforce, who in 1801 said, "I dare not marry . . . the future . . . is so unsettled," or as did William Pitt, who in 1806 said, "There is scarcely anything round us but ruin and despair." In the midst of staggering disillusionment, many cry for the bread of faith.

There is also a deep longing for the bread of hope. In the early years of this century many people did not hunger for this bread. The days of the first telephones, automobiles, and airplanes gave them a radiant optimism. They worshipped at the shrine of inevitable progress. They believed that every new scientific achievement lifted man to higher levels of perfection. But then a series of tragic developments, revealing the selfishness and corruption of man, illustrated with frightening clarity the truth of Lord Acton's dictum, "Power tends to corrupt and absolute power corrupts absolutely." This awful discovery led to one of the most colossal breakdowns of optimism in history. For so many people, young and old, the light of hope went out, and they roamed wearily in the dark chambers of pessimism. Many concluded that life has no meaning. Some agreed with the philosopher Schopenhauer that life is an endless pain with a painful end, and that life is a tragicomedy played over and over again with only slight changes in costume and scenery. Others cried out like Shakespeare's Macbeth, that life is a tale told by an idiot, full of sound and fury, signifying nothing.

But even in the inevitable moments when all seems hopeless, men know that without hope they cannot really live, and in agonizing desperation they cry for the bread of hope.

And there is the deep longing for the bread of love. Everybody wishes to love and to be loved. He who feels that he is not loved feels that he does not count. Much has happened in the modern world to make men feel that they do not belong. Living in a world that has become oppressively impersonal, many of us have come to feel that we are little more than numbers. Ralph Borsodi, in an arresting picture of a world wherein numbers have replaced persons, writes that the modern mother is often maternity case No. 8434 and her child, after being fingerprinted and footprinted, becomes No. 8003, and that a funeral in a large city is an event in Parlor B with Class B flowers and decorations at which Preacher No. 14 officiates and Musician No. 84 sings Selection No. 174. Bewildered by this tendency to reduce man to a card in a vast index, man desperately searches for the bread of love.

When the man in the parable knocked on his friend's door and asked for the three loaves of bread, he received the impatient retort, "Do not bother me; the door is now shut, and my children are with me in bed; I cannot get up and give you anything." How often have men experienced a similar disappointment when at midnight they knock on the door of the church. Millions of Africans, patiently knocking on the door of the Christian church where they seek the bread of social justice, have either been altogether ignored or told to wait until later, which almost always means never. Millions of American Negroes, starving for the want of the bread of freedom, have knocked again and again on the door of so-called white churches, but they have usually been greeted by a cold indifference or a blatant hypocrisy. Even the white religious leaders, who have a heartfelt desire to open the door and provide the bread, are often more cautious than courageous and more prone to follow the expedient than the ethical path. One of the shameful tragedies of history is that the very institution which should remove man from the midnight of racial segregation participates in creating and perpetuating the midnight.

In the terrible midnight of war, men have knocked on the door of the church to ask for the bread of peace, but the church has often disappointed them. What more pathetically reveals the irrelevancy of the church in present-day world affairs than its witness regarding war? In a world gone mad with arms buildups, chauvinistic passions, and imperialistic exploitation, the church has either endorsed these activities or remained appallingly silent. During the last two world wars, national churches even functioned as the ready lackeys of the state, sprinkling holy water upon the battleships and joining the mighty armies in singing, "Praise the Lord and pass the ammunition." A weary world, pleading desperately for peace, has often found the church morally sanctioning war.

And those who have gone to the church to seek the bread of economic justice have been left in the frustrating midnight of economic privation. In many instances the church has so aligned itself with the privileged classes and so defended the status quo that it has been unwilling to answer the knock at midnight. The Greek Church in Russia allied itself with the status quo and became so inextricably bound to the despotic czarist regime that it became impossible to be rid of the corrupt political and social system without being rid of the church. Such is the fate of every ecclesiastical organization that allies itself with things-as-they-are.

The church must be reminded that it is not the master or

the servant of the state, but rather the conscience of the state. It must be the guide and the critic of the state, and never its tool. If the church does not recapture its prophetic zeal, it will become an irrelevant social club without moral or spiritual authority. If the church does not participate actively in the struggle for peace and for economic and racial justice, it will forfeit the loyalty of millions and cause men everywhere to say that it has atrophied its will. But if the church will free itself from the shackles of a deadening status quo, and, recovering its great historic mission, will speak and act fearlessly and insistently in terms of justice and peace, it will enkindle the imagination of mankind and fire the souls of men, imbuing them with a glowing and ardent love for truth, justice, and peace. Men far and near will know the church as a great fellowship of love that provides light and bread for lonely travelers at midnight.

While speaking of the laxity of the church, I must not overlook the fact the so-called Negro church has also left men disappointed at midnight. I say so-called Negro church because ideally there can be no Negro or white church. It is to their everlasting shame that white Christians developed a system of racial segregation within the church, and inflicted so many indignities upon its Negro worshipers that they had to organize their own churches.

Two types of Negro churches have failed to provide bread. One burns with emotionalism, and the other freezes with classism. The former, reducing worship to entertainment, places more emphasis on volume than on content and confuses spirituality with muscularity. The danger in such a church is that the members may have more religion in their hands and feet than in their hearts and souls. At midnight this type of church has neither the vitality nor the relevant gospel to feed hungry souls.

The other type of Negro church that feeds no midnight traveler has developed a class system and boasts of its dignity, its membership of professional people, and its exclusiveness. In such a church the worship service is cold and meaningless, the music dull and uninspiring, and the sermon little more than a homily on current events. If the pastor says too much about Jesus Christ, the members feel that he is robbing the pulpit of dignity. If the choir sings a Negro spiritual, the members claim an affront to their class status. This type of church tragically fails to recognize that worship at its best is a social experience in which people from all levels of life come together to affirm their oneness and unity under God. At midnight men are altogether ignored because of their limited education, or they are given bread that has been hardened by the winter of morbid class-consciousness.

In the parable we notice that after the man's initial disappointment, he continued to knock on his friend's door. Because of his importunity—his persistence—he finally persuaded his friend to open the door. Many men continue to knock on the door of the church at midnight, even after the church has so bitterly disappointed them, because they know the bread of life is there. The church today is challenged to proclaim God's Son, Jesus Christ, to be the hope of men in all of their complex personal and social problems. Many will continue to come in quest of answers to life's problems. Many young people who knock on the door are perplexed by the uncertainties of life, confused by daily disappointments, and disillusioned by the ambiguities of history. Some who come have been taken from their schools and careers and cast in the role of soldiers. We must provide them with the fresh bread of hope and imbue them with the conviction that God has the power to bring good out of evil. Some who come are tortured by a nagging guilt resulting from their wandering in the midnight of ethical relativism and their surrender to the doctrine of self-expression. We must lead them to Christ who will offer them the fresh bread of forgiveness. Some who knock are tormented by the fear of death as they move toward the evening of life. We must provide them with the bread of faith in immortality, so that they may realize that this earthly life is merely an embryonic prelude to a new awakening.

Midnight is a confusing hour when it is difficult to be faithful. The most inspiring word that the church may speak is that no midnight long remains. The weary traveler by midnight who asks for bread is really seeking the dawn. Our eternal message of hope is that dawn will come. Our slave foreparents realized this. They were never unmindful of the fact of midnight, for always there was the rawhide whip of the overseer and the auction block where families were torn asunder to remind them of its reality. When they thought of the agonizing darkness of midnight, they sang:

> Oh, nobody knows de trouble I've seen,
> Glory Hallelujah!
> Sometimes I'm up, sometimes I'm down,
> Oh, yes, Lord,
> Sometimes I'm almost to de groun',
> Oh, yes, Lord,
> Oh, nobody knows de trouble I've seen,
> Glory Hallelujah!

Encompassed by a staggering midnight but believing that morning would come, they sang:

> I'm so glad trouble don't last always.
> O my Lord, O my Lord, what shall I do?

Their positive belief in the dawn was the growing edge of hope that kept the slaves faithful amid the most barren and tragic circumstances.

Faith in the dawn arises from the faith that God is good and just. When one believes this, he knows that the contradictions of life are neither final nor ultimate. He can walk through the dark night with the radiant conviction that all things work together for good for those that love God. Even the most starless midnight may herald the dawn of some great fulfillment.

At the beginning of the bus boycott in Montgomery, Alabama, we set up a voluntary car pool to get the people to and from their jobs. For eleven long months our car pool functioned extraordinarily well. Then Mayor Gayle introduced a resolution instructing the city's legal department to file such proceedings as it might deem proper to stop the operation of the car pool or any transportation system growing out of the bus boycott. A hearing was set for Tuesday, November 13, 1956.

At our regular weekly mass meeting, scheduled the night before the hearing, I had the responsibility of warning the people that the car pool would probably be enjoined. I knew that they had willingly suffered for nearly twelve months, but could we now ask them to walk back and forth to their jobs? And if not, would we be forced to admit that the protest had failed? For the first time, I almost shrank from appearing before them.

When the evening came, I mustered sufficient courage to tell them the truth. I tried, however, to conclude on a note of hope. "We have moved all of these months," I said, "in the daring faith that God is with us in our struggle. The many experiences of days gone by have vindicated that faith in a marvelous way. Tonight we must believe that a way will be made out of no way." Yet I could feel the cold breeze of pessimism pass over the audience. The night was darker than a thousand midnights. The light of hope was about to fade and the lamp of faith to flicker.

A few hours later, before Judge Carter, the city argued that we were operating a "private enterprise" without a franchise. Our lawyers argued brilliantly that the car pool was a voluntary "share-a-ride" plan provided without profit as a service by Negro churches. It became obvious that Judge Carter would rule in favor of the city.

At noon, during a brief recess, I noticed an unusual commotion in the courtroom. Mayor Gayle was called to the back room. Several reporters moved excitedly in and out of the room. Momentarily a reporter came to the table where, as chief defendant, I sat with the lawyers. "Here is the decision that you have been waiting for," he said. "Read this release."

In anxiety and hope, I read these words: "The United States Supreme Court today unanimously ruled bus segregation unconstitutional in Montgomery, Alabama." My heart throbbed with an inexpressible joy. The darkest hour of our struggle had become the first hour of victory. Someone shouted from the back of the courtroom, "God Almighty has spoken from Washington!"

The dawn will come. Disappointment, sorrow, and despair are born at midnight, but morning follows. "Weeping may endure for a night," says the psalmist, "but joy cometh in the morning." This faith adjourns the assemblies of hopelessness and brings new light into the dark chambers of pessimism.

4

The State of the Race and a Vision for the Future

HERBERT EATON

> But let judgment run down as waters, and righteousness as a mighty stream.
>
> Amos 5:24

Today, we gather to honor the memory and celebrate the legacy of the late Rev. Dr. Martin Luther King Jr. I cannot think of a more fitting way for us to honor him than to cite our profound debt of gratitude for his leadership by exploring the current status of the race, and by suggesting future directions for racial empowerment.

The Civil Rights Movement, led by Dr. King, resulted in the dismantling of many discrimination laws against blacks, which had been on the books for decades. These laws, and the humiliating behavior patterns associated with them, were directed against us with universal approval. They amounted to a national public policy against blacks.

Dr. King dreamed of the eradication of all laws which prevented blacks from enjoying free access to public places and public institutions. His was a call for an end to legal segregation. The laws were ultimately changed. Public places and public institutions did become desegregated. The question now is, to what extend did the welfare of the masses of black people change? Or, did their condition get worse?

Let's be candid! Conditions for the masses of blacks grew worse, because the Civil Rights Movement died with the assassination of Dr. King. Other groups arose demanding their civil rights, and black civil rights were drowned out by these new groups vying for their rights on the coat tails, suffering, and sacrifices of blacks. They called for women's rights, gay rights, Hispanic rights, Asian rights, poor whites' rights, and handicapped rights.

These groups, along with the conservatives, outflanked black leadership. Black leaders ran out of insight, social tools, and strategies for effectively dealing with the more subtle and less direct forms of racism that cropped up. The legitimate base of the black movement was diluted beyond recognition. Conservatives identified every group that could possibly perceive itself as being oppressed and made them equal to blacks. Thus, there was no further urgency to address black civil rights.

Today, the Urban League and the NAACP are still alive, but they have lost much of their influence and membership. The Student Non-Violent Coordinating Committee and the Black Panther party are defunct. The Congress of Racial Equality has joined the conservative ranks of a national political party, and the SCLC barely survives. The government disabled black civil rights groups by destroying black leadership.

Adam Clayton Powell and Stokeley Carmichael were discredited; Martin Luther King, Jr., Malcolm X, and Medgar Evers were assassinated; Rap Brown, Eldridge Cleaver, Angela

Herbert Eaton was born in Creedmoor, North Carolina. He earned the B.S. from North Carolina College at Durham and then the B.D. from the School of Religion at Howard University. He later received the S.T.M. from Boston University School of Theology. After further study at the University of Chicago, Reverend Eaton was awarded a Ford Foundation grant and studied African history and received the M.A. degree from Howard University. He was pastor of Dexter Avenue Baptist Church from 1960 to 1965. He was also pastor of Kenwood United Church of Christ, Chicago, Illinois; and director of the United Campus Christian Ministry, Durham, North Carolina. He now lives in Durham.

Davis and prominent members of the Black Panthers were criminalized. Most of the other black leaders ran for the protective cover offered by electoral politics. As black elected officials, they became champions for their political party and the American economic system, rather than championing the cause of the black community, while the conditions of those black masses who put them into office grew worse than before the Civil Rights Movement started.

For example, the Urban League reports that in 1964, there were only 103 black elected officials in America. During the same year, black unemployment was at 10.8 percent, and 33 percent of the prison population was black. Also, in 1964, 34 percent of blacks were below the poverty line economically and black per capita income was less than one half that of whites.

At the beginning of 1995, conditions for the masses of black people were even more bleak. The prediction was that with the hardening of the conservative stance, black life would get even worse. Clearly, most black public officials do not advocate for us, few can point to a program or policy that was enacted specifically and solely to relieve the horrendous conditions in black communities. . . . Yet, at nearly every level of government and in corporate America, there are some programs or policies that target women, Native Americans, Asians, Hispanics, the handicapped, and other aggrieved groups.

Once black public officials accepted the idea of supporting measures to assist everybody except blacks, they have eliminated the importance of having black elected officials. They sit there and pretend to be race-neutral while our race and our communities sink deeper into the quagmire of obsolescence.

How did we get into this mess?! First of all, the brightest and most objective minds among blacks, such as the Harvest Institute, a black think tank in Washington, and the African American Institute for Research and Empowerment in Boston, agree that blacks made a big mistake by focusing the entire weight of our resources on achieving integration. Clearly, integration has not worked for most blacks. Black leaders were naive to believe that by removing symbols of Jim Crowism and acquiring access to various segments of white society, black people would gain equality.

In his most recent book, *Black Labor: White Wealth*, Dr. Claud Anderson, founder of the Harvest Institute, states the unanimous position of the best of black minds: that real integration will never come true for blacks. And even if it did, it wouldn't change the quality of black life because all plans and goals would have to be processed through and approved by the dominant society. Therefore, integration, they insist, is a detriment to blacks, because the larger white society will never allow blacks to assimilate nor help blacks to alter the negative marginal conditions in which we live by encouraging the creation of organized group wealth and organized group power.

A strong emphasis of integration requires that blacks give up their culture, their values, and all that is identifiably black. Thus, such an integration process is divisive and detrimental to black self-empowerment goals because it dilutes and fragments our numerical strength. Even worse, blacks are forced to shape their goals, values, and behavior around white America's standards.

Secondly, along with the myth of integration, the twin myth of "equal opportunity for all" has also contributed to our predicament. We black Americans devote a significant amount of time and energy chasing the myth of equal opportunity. Inequality of power and wealth will always exist so long as human greed and competition motivate human behavior. This myth of "equal opportunity for all" not only keeps blacks distracted from learning how to increase and activate our organized group wealth and our organized group power, but it keeps us believing that at least our children or our children's children will have a fair chance at being accepted in white society

We must grow to see that pursuing the concept of equality, rather than organized group wealth and organized group power, is another quagmire that bogs us down and wastes time, energy, and efforts.

Other influences contributing to our condition are the legal system, the absence of group economics, and the ongoing efforts at criminalizing blacks, especially black males.

Now let us consider some reasonable and responsible recommendations that we need to embrace to improve the quality of black life and black communities. First, a great writer once said that, "those whom the gods would make powerful must first organize." Few words could be truer for blacks! Whether individual blacks believe in integration, segregation, or moderation, we must all come together around the goals of improving the living conditions of our race. Although our politics and our philosophy may differ, all blacks are united by the color of our skin, and the consequences of living in black skin.

Therefore, when we organize, we cannot afford to close the door to any black person regardless of his or her economic condition, educational accomplishments, social status, religious or sexual orientation, political commitment, personal life-style, or anything else. In such a grouping, great sensitivity and tact will be required of those convening organizational meetings. We must not permit name-calling or putting each other down. We must be open to listen to and respect all opinions. We must also be patient with each other. We must insist on the putting aside of all selfish agendas, and focus on what is best for the race in every discussion.

In our organizational meetings, we must be open to the emergence of other leaders than those the community traditionally looks to for leadership. To this end, we must work at developing a cadre of new leaders from all segments of the community. The organized group power of which I speak is the most important ingredient in the advancement of any race. In organizing, we must remember to think strategically at all levels of decision making.

The second recommendation has to do with the acquisition of group wealth. When considered as a nation within a nation, black Americans are not poor. The latest, most responsible government statistics reveal that black Americans have approximately $280 billion annually of disposable income. This is more money than the annual budget of Canada and most third world countries. But, as a group, we are extremely impoverished because we have not learned how to make our money work for us. We have failed to create our own internal economy. We do not allow our dollars to exchange hands in the black community. Less than 1 percent of our money is spent with black business. Over 99 percent is spent empowering and enriching those outside our community.

To develop economically, black dollars must bounce eight to ten times before leaving the black community. Contained and recirculated dollars within black communities would stimulate business, create employment opportunities and expand tax bases. By spending most of our money with non-black businesses, blacks deprive their communities of a tax base providing human services as well as jobs. Thus, blacks actually disempower themselves.

The final recommendation for improving the condition of the race pertains to political activities among blacks. For black public officials, the most important issue must not be which political party one belongs to. Nor must it be the priorities of the party while whites switch political parties at the blink of an eye to make their bottom line come out right.

During slavery, blacks didn't belong to any political party, From the end of the Civil War until after the Great Depression, blacks primarily belonged to the Republican Party because Lincoln was a Republican. Still, we were subordinated, lynched, and segregated as a matter of national public policy.

From the late 1940s until today, about 85 percent of all registered black voters have been Democrats, Black Americans are still excluded and subordinated. This tells us that regardless of the degree of black involvement, black conditions remain unchanged. Therefore, in the opinion of many thoughtful black scholars, we ought to consider starting our own independent political party and run our own candidates for public office.

By creating our own independent black political organization, we would have little to lose since very few black public office holders win elections on the white vote. If nothing else, an independent black political party would get blacks public forums, financial support, and candidates committed to the black community, and whites will respect them for having some backbone. Why not go for it?!

Let me share with you a personal experience. My wife and I recently participated in a national black leadership conference in Baltimore. The focus of the conference was the urgency of creating a national black independent political party. The State of the Race Conference was financed by the Black United Fund and seven other progressive black organizations. It was attended by hundreds of highly resourceful and brilliant black persons, and the leadership was outstanding. Several black elected officials were invited to share in the deliberations. Not a single one showed up. All claimed prior commitments.

The truth of the matter is that they would not come to meet with us because they didn't want to offend their white financial supporters, and they didn't want to give the appearance of not supporting the priorities of the Democratic party. If we had our own strong internal economy, black candidates would not be held hostage by white institutions of wealth and power. We could finance our own candidates whose commitment would be totally to the black community.

Imagine what it would mean if African Americans could build independent black political organizations, community by community, country by country, all across America to harness our political power, based on collective community goals and interests. We would not be taken for granted, and we would be highly respected by all groups. The net result would be forward progress at an accelerated pace for all African Americans. We must build this independent black political organization based on the axiom, "No permanent friends, no permanent enemies, just permanent interests."

We must accept this challenge as a sacred obligation and memorial to the millions of black Africans who died in that dreaded middle passage to the New World. We must do it in memory of thousands of other Africans who were brutalized, maimed, tortured, and murdered through over 250 years of the most inhumane slavery system known to mankind.

This independent black political organization will likewise fulfill the highest aspirations of all of our trailblazers since emancipation, and it will make more secure the future well-being of our grandchildren.

It is then that we can unite our spirits with the spirits of our ancestors, and with the spirit of Dr. King, Jr., as we join them in singing, "Free at last, free at last, free at last, thank God almighty, we are free at last!!!"

5

Needed: An Enduring Courtship

G. Murray Branch

> Therefore, behold, I will allure her, and bring her into
> the wilderness, and speak tenderly to her, And there I
> will give her her vineyards, and make the valley of
> Achor a door of hope. And there she shall answer as in
> the days of her youth, as at the time when
> she came out of the land of Egypt.
> *Hosea 2:14,15 (RSV)*

Marriage and hanging go by destiny; matches are made in heaven." So wrote an English clergyman and man of letters in a work once widely read called "The Anatomy of Melancholy" and which appeared in 1621.

In these days one never hears the first part of the statement quoted, although the second part remains in circulation and gains increased attention during the month of June.

All societies consider marriage to be a joyous occasion and in all ancient societies it was a religious rite involving both solemn ceremony and joyful celebration. In Roman Catholic and Orthodox Church circles marriage is still a religious happening—a sacrament. But in general, civil marriages have increased in numbers as modern life has become more secularized.

For this and other reasons the institution of marriage as we know it is in grave difficulty. Many innovations and adjustments are being proposed and tried—trial marriage, group marriage, wife- and husband-swapping, and so on. We may not expect any return to health and sanity for marriage and the family unless we reassert in this society and make prevail an understanding of marriage which transcends mere whim or fancy or economic or physiological convenience.

It may not be necessary to link marriage with hanging as predestined, but matches must be viewed as made in heaven, that is, as belonging to the ongoing purpose of God to build community and to establish a society of justice, harmony, and peace in the world.

Seven centuries before Christ, the prophet Hosea introduced courtship and marriage as an analogy of the relationship between the Lord and his people Israel. Because Israel had been unfaithful to the covenant, had broken the marriage bond, and had gone aside into the way of adultery, the prophet, discerning the divine intention, announced on the Lord's behalf a renewal of courtship as recorded in Hosea 2:14-15 (see opening of this sermon).

Hosea was convinced that the Lord is a God of steadfast love who refuses to disown his chosen bride even though unfaithful.

How can I give you up, O Ephraim! How can I hand you over, O Israel! How can I make you like Admah! How can I treat you like Zeboiim! My heart recoils within me, my

G. Murray Branch was born in Prince Edward County, Virginia, in 1914. He is a graduate of Virginia Union University (B.S., 1939, cum laude), and Andover Newton Theological School (B.D., 1941). He served as field secretary of the National Council of the Young Men's Christian Association (1944-47) before beginning his teaching career at Morehouse College. Dr. Branch was instrumental in the founding of the Interdenominational Theological Center, Atlanta, Georgia. He was called to the Dexter pulpit not once but twice, serving from 1966–1972, and again from 1977–1989.

compassion grows warm and tender. I will not execute my
fierce anger, I will not again destroy Ephriam; for I am God
and not man, the Holy One in your midst . . . Hosea 11:8-9

The prophet's understanding that divine love endures,
reclaims and restores prompted him to relate in similar fashion
to his own unfaithful wife. He perceived that "matches are
made in heaven." The groom takes the initiative and establishes
with Israel his chosen bride *an Enduring Courtship.*

Just as in the days of Hosea and in the northern Hebrew
kingdom there was need for an enduring courtship, so also in
our own time and in America there is needed *an enduring
courtship.* Now, however, the heavenly groom has come closer
to earth in the person of Christ and the bride is nearer at hand
in the Church. Yet there is today no less alienation, no less
estrangement than in Hosea's time. The Bride of Christ has
gone astray, whoring after worthless lovers no less than did the
ancient people of God.

What is it that causes marriages to go on the rocks? The
answer is clear; there is no mystery here. Unfaithfulness, disloy-
alty, breaking of covenant, incompatibility, hypocrisy, false-
hood, deceit, misplacement of values, adultery—the very patterns of behavior which marked Israel's relations with her Lord
and which today mark the relations of many a church to Christ.

The Church by definition is a community of believers in the
Lordship of Jesus Christ, but there is little *koinonia*—fellowship or participation or mutuality within the body and little
faith in the Christ's sovereignty or providence. We want to do
it ourselves and intend to do it our way.

The Church is by God's choice a called-out people who
have been baptized by the Holy Spirit, reconciled to God, set

apart, nurtured unto sanctification in order to be a people peculiar to God and witnessing for God in the world. But our witness is more for Wall Street or the State Department or the American Way or Southern Tradition.

The Church is the saved and saving remnant through which the Grace of the Eternal may be mediated to needy and troubled humanity. But so many bodies calling themselves churches are self-perpetuating, self-directing, and self-serving, while the creation grows and travails for the manifestation of the sons of God.

A few weeks ago Christians observed Pentecost, the birthday of the church, but it was for the most part only a perfunctory anniversary celebration, a time for sentimentality and indulgence of appetite with little or no thought given to how it may recapture the unity, the singleness of purpose, the fervent appeal and transforming power which changed the course of history when the Spirit was poured out in that Jerusalem Upper Room long ago.

Nevertheless, and despite our having forsaken Christ in favor of idol gods, the Lord carries on *an enduring courtship* with his Church because he is the exemplary heavenly groom whose loving kindness faileth never and whose priority is to reclaim and to restore his bride, wayward though she be.

> Therefore, I will allure her, and bring her into the wilderness and speak tenderly to her. And there I will give her her vineyards, and make the valley of Achor a door of hope. And there she shall answer as in the days of her youth as at the time when she came out of the land of Egypt.

A wilderness is a desert, a wild, uncultivated region. We are wont to think of such a barren place as an unlikely locus for courtship. A garden or park is well suited for wooing, but hardly a desert. Yet it was in the deserts of Sinai and Paran that the extraordinary courtship began between this God of the wilds and this semi-nomadic, underdeveloped people. Hosea had heard of the forty years his ancestors had spent in this wilderness training ground under the leadership of Moses. It was then that the Covenant was established at Sinai and the Israelites learned through hard experience how to do for themselves while at the same time to depend on God for both guidance and support.

It seems to be a universal and timeless fact of human experience that privations, hardships, insecurity, etc., produce the keenest insights and develop the strongest God-consciousness. Recall the Pilgrim Fathers who settled on these shores, three and a half centuries ago. By contrast, prosperity, abundance, and comfort readily lead to gluttony, dullness of mind, faltering social concern, and withering of spiritual sensitivity. "Woe to them that are at ease in Zion" was a pronouncement made by Amos, Hosea's prophet contemporary.

The elect society then or now is not immune to corruption and decay which follow in the wake of superficial thinking and sensate living. So the wilderness is the best place for God to speak to the heart of his chosen. There, the text tells us, the husbandman par excellence will cultivate vineyards for his beloved, vineyards which will be heavy with fruit for the spirit and from which will be tread out wine, not to make merry the heart just for a season, but to make the whole of life a continuing celebration and marriage festival.

There is evidence about us today suggesting that the Church is experiencing an era of intensified courtship. For a generation or more the church has reposed in what Harold Cooke Phillips of Cleveland calls the "lap of luxury," which is too comfortable a state from which to be easily aroused. The driving summons to duty has not been getting through to us.

But fresh breezes are now blowing across the world. "The answer is blowing in the wind." And the church has felt the effect. A second Pentecost may well be upon us. Vatican II prayed for it, but most churchmen were surprised and not a little perplexed, even outdone, when the Spirit was poured out so suddenly and so profusely and was not confined to *established* churches.

It is a hard lesson for "successful" people to learn that the transforming Spirit of God cannot be programmed by man, even by those of us who purport to be the Bride of Christ. The Lord of heaven and earth does his own courting, his own choosing, his own proposing.

The Church's part is to answer "as in the days of her youth," as at the time when she came out of Greco-Roman bondage. Those were days of persecution, imprisonment, martyrdom. Never forget that the cross is the Church's chief symbol—not a cross of silver or gold, polished and bejeweled, but a rough-hewn tree, an instrument of ignominy and shame, an officially authorized device for murder and suppression of both political and religious dissent.

But the cross, though intended as an instrument of defeat and death, God made into a sign of life and hope surpassing even the promise God made through Hosea concerning the valley of Achor.

If there is to be hope or promise in the Christian Church today, she must respond to her Lord as she did in the days of her youth. This involves a twofold responsibility: worship and work, to be alone with Christ and to be in the world for Christ. There must be this alternation between apartness and involvement—the gathered Church and the scattered Church.

We come together as now on the Lord's day for worship, for communion, for mediation, for fellowship, for replenishment, for occasional correction, for checking our orders, and perhaps for reassignment. We depart to serve, to witness, to evangelize, to teach, to extend a helping hand to the faltering and the needy, a world of love to the friendless and lonely, of encouragement to the despondent and the oppressed, to say to all and sundry who struggle for abundant life, "Look us, take heart, Right on! There is an *enduring courtship* carried on by the Lord with his Church."

> O Love that wilt not let me go.
> I rest my weary soul in Thee;
> I give thee back the life I owe,
> That in Thine ocean depths its flow
> May richer, fuller be.
>
> O Cross that liftest up my head,
> I dare not ask to fly from Thee;
> I lay in dust life's glory dead,
> And from the ground there blossoms red
> Life that shall endless be.
>
> Geo. Matheson

6

What Are You Doing Here?

ROBERT M. DICKERSON, JR.

> O come, let us sing unto the Lord: let us make a joyful
> noise to the rock of our salvation . . . In his hand are
> the deep places of the earth: the strength of the hills is
> his also . . . O come, let us worship and bow down: let
> us kneel before the Lord our maker.
>
> *Psalm 95: 1-6*

A fellow thought his girlfriend was two-timing him, so he rushed to her apartment one afternoon, stormed up the stairs where she was living, burst through the door, and said, "Where is he? Where is he? Where is that other guy you've been fooling around with?" She said, "What do you mean?" He said, "I want to know where that other guy is you've been fooling around with?" She said, "I don't know." He looked over and the window was open, and the curtain blowing out. So he rushed over to the window, looked down, and there was a guy running along the ground below. In a rage he grabbed a refrigerator and threw it out the window at him, breaking window frame and all. The exertion was so great, it caused him to have a heart seizure, and he died. Later, the Apostle Peter was letting three dead men into Heaven. He looked at the first guy and said, "What are you doing here?" And he said, "Aw, I thought my girlfriend was two-timing me, and I went over to her apartment, and I saw a guy running along the ground below, and I threw a refrigerator at him, and it killed me." Peter turned to the second guy and said, "What are you doing here?" He said, "I don't know. I was late to my shift this afternoon and was running across the yard of my apartment, and I got hit by something." Peter turned to the third guy. He said, "What are you doing here?" He said, "I don't have any idea. I was sitting in a refrigerator minding my own business!"

What are you doing here? I would like to think that we could take inventory now before readings, papers, and assorted other assignments clog our thinking apparatus. But why are you here or what are you doing here? I'd like to think you've come to learn.

In the first place I hope we have come to learn the Book. One of the problems that puzzles me after years of preaching is that we have some in our ranks who ignore that admonition of the Lord that we're to love him with all our mind. They put a lot of emphasis upon the heart and soul, but through dedicated ignorance and consecrated blunders they consider they're serving the Lord.

As I interpret it, love for God, and devotion to the truth, and submission to the Holy Spirit are all features of a mature Christian life. On the basis of Christ's teaching, I think it is an inescapable fact and a part of our Christian commitment to think out our Christian faith and the significance of it and how it relates to our present-day dilemma. Now a spin-off of this

Robert M. Dickerson was born in Pine Bluff, Arkansas, where he received his early education. He is a graduate of University of Arkansas at Pine Bluff with a major in pre-medicine. He was called to the ministry in 1967 and attended the Southwestern Baptist Theological Seminary in Fort Worth, Texas, where he received the Master of Divinity degree in 1970. He earned a doctorate from the Phillips Graduate Seminary in Enid, Oklahoma, in 1974. Dr. Dickerson has had many professional positions within the African American church. He served as pastor of the Dexter Avenue Baptist Church 1973–1977. Currently he is the pastor of the historic First African Baptist Church, Columbus, Georgia.

thing is to search out the most effective means of advancing the cause of Christ in our day. We need to develop a more convincing way of presenting the gospel. We must make the Bible come alive and be contemporary as it speaks to men, listening forever to the voice of men as they cry back to a searching Father.

There are so many hearts and lives that need to be healed today. And only God can heal those people, but in his game plan, he uses you and me. His healing does not come apart from his truth that shines as a new light out of the pages of the Bible. Listen to what the writer of Hebrews said:

> For the word of God is living, and active, and sharper than any two-edge sword, and piercing as far as in the division of the soul and spirit, of both the joints and marrow, and able to judge the thoughts and the intentions of the heart. (Hebrews 4:12)

But how are we presenting the Bible? Have we been guilty, as one layman charged, of presenting the Bible as a great wall that is fixed between now and then, holding little or no relevance to today without any handles for the 1987 man, or have we been guilty of presenting the Bible as a kind of vapid or stale latter-day morality with no integrity or authority? One of these views is too "other worldly." And the other is too "this worldly," and somewhere in between these two extremes we must work. There can be no lasting Church renewal without Biblical renewal. This comes by knowing the scriptures. You can no more preach or teach that which you do not know than you can come back from where you ain't been.

What are you doing here? I hope you're here to know and to

sincerely and conscientiously attempt to analyze and understand and interpret the Bible and heed what Paul said, "Study
to show thyself approved unto God, a workman unashamed,
rightly dividing the word of truth." (Timothy 2:15) Let's dig
deeper into the Bible; let's seek it; let's search it; let's sift it; let's
wait for the Lord to grant us a greater insight. Now this is not
to deprecate the fields other than the Biblical but to undergird
our total theological education with every skill beginning with
"The Book." You're not effective as a preacher unless you know
how to teach. You're not effective as a teacher unless you've got
some theology. You're not an effective musician unless you can
do something other than heist a tune.

What are you doing here? If you're here simply to limit
yourself to knowing "The Book," I feel sorry for you.

I hope that in the second place, you've come to learn to live
with yourself. And in the words of Bill Shakespeare, "Ay, there's
the rub." Vocational Christian workers are, for the most part, a
strange lot. But if we're going to be effective ministers, I think
we've got to deal with ourselves. To have only Biblical knowledge, even a seminary degree, while at the same time be fraught
with personality quirks and a poor self-image is to negate all
your effectiveness. Your ability to function is not your education in your head, but it is your education with yourself and
with others. The presence of phonies and role-playing and
Halloweening it 365 days of the year is less than sub-Christian.

Coming to live with oneself begins by honestly looking at
ourselves—taking off our masks. This means we must be
honest. The conscious and unconscious feelings that you have
about yourself constitute your self-image. And you will act out
in life, in harmony, how you view yourself. The Bible recognized this in Proverbs when it said, "For as he thinketh in his

heart, so is he," or in other words, whatever you feel yourself to be at the center of your emotional nature, that is what you really are, existentially, and your actions will be in harmony with your own self-concept. Now, because far too many vocational Christian workers have a poor self-image, we see the result of this in our work—a pastor becomes a dictator; a staff member becomes insecure; the education person isn't willing to be second fiddle; the minister of music acts like a prima donna, and the director of children's work acts like the proverbial old maid, all because of self-image problems.

I'd like to be positive by saying that we're too negative about ourselves. Herb Barks said it, "God don't make no junk." However, to be truly open to yourself, you must be willing to look within—come to say, "I like me; I like the way I am." Accept yourself as you are. Now this is not resignation, but it's wise insight into reality. Now the trick is to see that part of your life which is hidden from you. Unless we see and accept ourselves as we truly are we build layers and layers of all kinds of false covers hiding our own true selves from ourselves as well as others. God thought enough of us to send Jesus because He thought we were worth saving, and we must find self-respect if we are to be a whole person. He did not say, "Come unto me and get it over with." But he said, "Come join my school and learn of me." Give God not just what you are, but what you can become. The real difficulty in being open to ourselves is our pride—pride that overrides even our common sense sometimes.

What are you doing here? I hope you've come to learn to live with yourself. I hope you've come to learn to live with others. Now if the first two points are preaching with little or no meddling then it comes here. The goal of a Christian is to be perfect and this goal does not stop with personal development but also relates to our horizontal relationships between our fellowman where we're also to be mature and to be responsible. We're to accept people as our equals and worthy of our love. There is a stupendous need for human relations on this "Holy Hump." Jesus aimed at developing mature disciples who were a community of learners—able to stand on their feet with mutual respect and love for one another. He tried to jar them out of their slave mentality when he said, "I do not call you slaves any longer . . . I call you friends . . . and I command you to love one another."

What are you doing here? I hope you're here to learn to live with others. If we allow such conduct of hostility, and antagonism, and aggression and condescending attitudes to develop here among the schools, we only create new problems that extend themselves out to the local churches where a pastor, a minister of education, a minister of music, and a director of children's work are to be out there—where the pastor is the quarterback, not the coach. Lest I be misunderstood, let me assure you my emphasis here is preventative. However, on the other hand, I would be less than honest if I ignored some problem areas about living with others. Since there are sensitive areas and because my own heart's desire is to be redemptive, I will simply raise some points to ponder. Is there any place here for a condescending attitude on the part of a professor toward a student? Is there any place for an antagonistic student who would maliciously try to discredit a teacher? Is there any place for a person, either administration or faculty, who would have little trust in the other, in feeling that one is lazy and not as committed as I am? Is there any place for jealousy and envy among the single student over dating and friendship that could lead to romance if others would leave their jealous thoughts out?

What are you doing here? The last thing I want to say is this. I hope you've come to learn to be servants. You remember the story. It takes place when Jesus ate with His disciples for the last time. They had come to the table, the disciples somewhat angry and hostile one toward the other because there had been a power struggle taking place among the twelve disciples as to which position they would occupy in the Kingdom. So as they were seated around the table, some of them still concerned about the problem that they faced, no one speaking, it was Jesus who got up and took the towel and began to perform the task of washing their feet. This was the custom of that day because a traveler who had traveled any distance on the hot, dusty roads would always have his feet washed before a meal.

In this story, we have a study in miniature of Jesus's fundamental attitude toward life. All through the Gospels, you will see Christ serving, not being served. You see Him coming into the world in an act of condescension, leaving Heaven in all of its glory, taking upon Himself the form of a man, becoming obedient to death, even to the death of the cross (which was the death of a criminal).

Not only do we see His coming into the world in the role of a servant, but all the way from Bethlehem to Golgotha He is seen in the same role. Though a star flashed across the sky signaling His birth, it was in a stable He was born. You see Him astounding the teachers and professors in the temple; you later see Him with his parents, Mary and Joseph (common folk). You see Him when He could have turned stones into bread and fed Himself; He did not. But you do see Him turning the water to wine for someone else. This He did. You see Him when He should have worn a crown of royalty, choosing rather a crown of thorns.

Then on the Mount of Transfiguration, He refused to ascend into Heaven between two saints, but chose rather to die on a cross between two criminals. You see in the life of Christ this fundamental attitude of giving of himself in service. We have so missed the point of the washing of the feet. So many have seen it as an act that should be done today in some symbolic way, but what Jesus was trying to say to us was not symbolism; it was something that we must do in life—serving one another and our fellow man. Being servants!

The church is continuously gathering around the table and remembering the spiritual benefits of our Lord, but we have long ago laid aside the towel of service. The Church has had difficulty in integrating the two—serving mankind and continuing the spiritual aspects of Christianity. On the other hand, we have worshipped God, we have talked about the eternal spiritual values of the Christian life, to the exclusion of the fundamental basic needs of man in life. What a tragedy either position presents us—to the world of which we are part. For Jesus did not leave one off to accept the other, nor did He accept one to the exclusion of the other. Jesus took the towel as well as the cup and the bread. So here in this act of washing of the feet of the disciples, you will see Jesus's attitude toward life.

We also have here a study in miniature of what the Church was meant to be. Jesus is telling us that the mission of the Church is one of the selfless services to the world in the name of Christ. The Church is not in the world to be served, but to serve. And we are to be its servants.

The towel in some ways is a more relevant symbol for the Christian life than the cross. We have left off the towel, but, oh, how we need both! We sing that there is a cross for everyone. Well, this may not necessarily be true, but for the Christian there is a towel for everyone. Christ may not call upon all of us to die, but He does call upon all of us to serve. The Church needs to get back to this symbol for her life—the towel.

Jesus took a towel! Would you agree that the towel is not too conspicuous in the life of the church today? The masses outside the Church fail to see the towel in our hands. They do not see us as being ready to serve. Most of us have not come with a towel of service. Look at the attitude of Jesus. His attitude toward service was not commanding service, but giving. It was being a servant. I call upon you to pick up the towel again. We must! We must if we are to come to grips with what it means to be a servant. We must begin to get away from the idea of what others can do for us in keeping our little egos intact. We must come to the point of being a minister in the world today. There is really no reason or need in being disciples unless we understand the symbol of the towel.

There are all kinds of people hurting, needing our care, needing us to take the towel. In a world of flux and change, we must be change agents.

We are living in mean days—we are living in times when men will do anything to one another. Men (and women) will kill you, gossip about you, lie on you, do anything they think they are big enough to do. Talk about change—where is the time when the little courtesies mean something, like "thank you," "forgive me," "I'm sorry," "please." Yes, we are living in a day of change. How do we deal with this . . . well, Romans 8:28 tells us even the meanness and the joy we have will be worked to God's glory.

We live in a world still diseased with economic, racial, and social oppression it seems will never end. There is a need for change. Can we accept the challenge to make it better?

In a world where most of the people are hungry, most of the people are poor, most of the people colored (not white or black, but colored), and most of the people have never heard of the gospel of the risen Lord and Savior, will it continue to be business as usual?

In this world which is divided at its core—a divided world, divided homes, split and divided churches, divided in our attitudes—those of us who call ourselves "born again believers in Christ" fight with one another, fuss with one another, backbite one another—oh, what a challenge we face. Then we wonder why the spirit of God is not within our midst! Oh, yes, our world is broken and divided. Where is our towel?

What are you doing here? What about accepting the challenge to meet this head on and commit ourselves to change, to take the towel?

I am well aware that one does not have to be listed in "Who's Who" to know "What's What" in today's world. We do live in a shaky and hurting world. A world divided and shaken and hurting to its very foundation.

We live in a world . . . where missiles are guided and men misguided . . . where truth parades around in clothing of lies and misrepresentation . . . where in 1993 over two million of our people were arrested, or filed for divorce, or paid no income taxes.

Yes, there is a brokenness, division in our world. Yes, we have the habit in the brokenness of our world to measure men and women according to our own standards. We judge and measure a person by how tall he is from his feet to his head.

We measure others by the kind of clothes they wear, by the

kind of car they drive, by the kind of house they live in, by the king of neighborhood they live in, by the color of skin in which their soul is wrapped!

But I'm here to tell us today that we are not to measure man by how tall he is, but by the depth of his soul! God does not measure us because of the clothes on our back but because of the cloak of righteousness that hides the nakedness of our sins!

We are thinking about Mars and the other planets and possibly will soon talk to somebody who lives on another world . . . and, we don't even know how to talk to the person who lives next door—or even in our own house.

We are talking about singing in that great heavenly choir, and on Sunday morning there are people in our choir who can sing duets and warm us up but they won't speak to one another after the benediction!

We've got our deep freezer full of food, but our soul is hungry...We have our wall-to-wall carpets in our rooms, but the floors of our souls are bare and naked. We look at life as problems to be solved instead of a mystery to be lived.

We have our money, our two cars, our large houses, our large church budgets, and our churches filled on Sunday morning, but I declare unto us today, if we don't look at us on the inside we are going to be declared morally bankrupt. We are living in the last days. The great question, then, in light of all this is, what are we to do in reconciling, in bringing people together.

So I conclude with my first question: *Why are you here?* My prayer and dream is that you're here to learn to live with "The Book," but also to learn to live with yourself and to learn to live with others, and to learn to be servants.

Some of you have been throwing refrigerators in anger.

Some of you've been hit by them. And there's a lot of you been sitting in them. Maybe our prayer should be, "Lord, cool some of us down. Lord heal some of us. Lord, get some of us out of cold storage."

What are you doing here?!

7

Direction from the Foundation

BOYKIN SANDERS

Help carry one another's burdens, and in this
way you will obey the law of Christ.
Galatians 6:2 (Good News Bible)

I n Milton's *Paradise Lost* there is clear indication that
God's plan for the whole of creation fell short, that chaos
looms and grows on the landscape. And this perspective
emanated from Milton's own experiences. Out of a life of
misery and aborted expectations both in his own personal
questing and in his not-so-hopeful encounters within the
church and the world, Milton was forced to describe life's
defections as Satan, as forces against the Lord's intent for us and
the world. . . . This was his way of focusing on the drift away
from our potential. This was his way of indicating that we come
short of our best, that we are far off the mark of innocence, and
that the ennobling and heeding life is not automatic even when
we appeal to social advantages and to our religious or theological acumen. And yet behind and beyond all this drifting away
is the reminding scene of our first parents, our ancestors,

Boykin Sanders was born in South Carolina. He is a graduate of
Morris College (B.S., mathematics); Interdenominational Theo-
logical Center (M. Div.); and Harvard University (M.A., Ph.D.).
At Harvard, he concentrated in New Testament and Christian
Origins. Dr. Sanders was an assistant professor before coming to
Dexter where he served as pastor from 1990–1991. He currently
serves as Professor of New Testament and Greek at Virginia
Union School of Theology.

looking back to Eden to our first world of innocence. They gaze
on the best from a distance of shame and regret. They view with
their own eyes the beauty of things and beings. They savor the
sight of interlocking consciousness, of friendship, of remem-
brance, and of divine visits and chats as personal friends and
keepers of the intended order. But the foundation is no longer
there for them. Nor is it there for us. Innocence is spent. Wrong
is old. The night is long.

Over the distance of this loss, however, in the far recesses of
memory even now is the reminder of Paradise on the pages of
the Biblical tradition—on some pages more boldly sketched
than others. Nevertheless, they all in one way or another push
us towards a desired future by reminding us along the journey
that our vision is not strong enough for what we really want to
see and claim as our own. In the New Testament this comes to
focus in the words of Jesus regarding what the Kingdom of God
is like. From the prophets of old it is indicated in their calls for
justice, in their insistence that the weak be rescued from the
grips of those armed with the powers of this world, and
particularly through the cry of that prophet who hoped that the
rough would smooth out. In Martin Luther King, Jr., the
desired future comes in the perennial question "Where Do We
Go From Here?" with space allowed for yet another critical
concern "Chaos or Community?" And in Paul while viewing a
not-so-inviting scene in the Galatian community it came in the
directive "Help carry one another's burdens . . ." as a counter
directive to those who had begun to think that their way was
God's way.

And what is afoot in each instance is the crippling idea (and
even the practice) that the Divine is no larger than our political,
cultural and religious constructs, yes, no bigger than havens we

construct to manage life in accordance with outcomes that serve us best. For Paul tells us, as he did the Galatians, that we too often settle for less than what God wants from us and of us in the worst of times, simply because we are unwilling to embrace and fulfill the expectations of the life that we know is possible.

Yet in the midst of our failings—sometimes due to our own religious orientations, sometimes due to our desire to appear to be more than we really are, as our text suggests—there are reminders of what is best. In view of a worldliness that parades about under the claim of Biblical ties and Biblical sponsorship, in view of a culture that hates self-examination and a Church that is as guilty as the world around it for participating in and promoting unjust outcomes, I propose here a different consciousness. Here I believe that our help and fix must come from outside of our own cultural and political concoctions if we are at all interested in what we ought to be doing, where we ought to be going, and what future we ought to be planning. For the apostle, as if he could see our struggles throughout the ages of the world, directions come in his own words regarding the non-determinative nature of circumcision and non-circumcision. In his denial of power to both categories there comes forth an everlasting reminder that what is lost to us today is creation, what Paul calls a new creation, which I call here paradise. I want to tag it that way because Paul is referring, by use of the new creation language, to the foundation of the world, without which foundation our worlds become unacceptable expressions. And so Paul advised "Help carry one another's burdens . . ." from the foundation. This is an acceptable undertaking in the sight of the Almighty.

For me this means that we must look in the direction of

paradise, not to the good old days of America, for enduring concepts and for perspectives on what we are. We must look even through the eyes of our first Biblical parents, Adam and Eve, to the primordial life for what we must be and for solutions to long-standing issues. And what is the most pressing image there? For me what is most pressing and impressive there is the image of life that blossoms and looms outside of Satan's grasp. I find there an image of life outside of our worst selves. I detect there the unbroken state and a world of reality allowing no room for abuse and pain. I find how small I am in the scheme of things. I find no foolishness there.

In our look back we see no tears of our making, no conflict, no death, no environmental destruction, no racism, no worry, no suffering, no concept of suffering that many of us have taken as a requirement of true faith. We only hear of the wonderful story of how God would come personally to a garden world to chat with Adam and Eve in the cool of the day and how one could visually see the voice of God walking in the garden. We hear of no bigots, no oppressors, and no hard-of-hearing people. We hear of none disabled by human miscalculations and misadventures. We find no hegemonic plans.

And we hear of no warnings there. There is no threat of a divine sphere against a more earthly one. We hear of no need of the Divine to urge us on by suspending the rains of the heavens or reminding us through whirlwinds, dark clouds, storms, plagues, earthquakes, prophets, saviors, wars, diseases, strikes, or through the plots and ploys of other demonstrations. Nor do we hear as in our text of the tenuous position of those who unwisely seek to fool God: "Do not deceive yourselves; no one makes a fool of God. You will reap exactly what you plant." (Galatians 6:7)

No! No! None of this is there. These all belong to the works of diminished beings and calls to quit in the face of more threatening judgments.

But what is there? What can be seen when we turn our gaze there? We truly find the response of the morning. When we look to Paradise, to Eden or to Creation we focus on things that remind us of transcendence. We envision life in harmonious terms. We find justice diminished and work to revive it. We observe and become observers of the friendships of things and beings. There the lamb lies down with the lion. We find "togetherness" as the password for remapping and remaking the world. We find it to be the key to eternity. We find Paul's Galatian word, "Love your neighbor as you love yourself." We find hanging together counts. We find it to have a divine ring. We find the fulfillment of Paradise: "Help carry the burdens of one another, and in this way you will obey the law of Christ."

As we move away from the image of Paradise we experience another image. This time it is Jesus, the crucified one. We see that the cross is Paradise, too. Yet we are most troubled by that association since the cross is so much unlike the pristine images of Eden. However, it is just like it and more in the end. As the password of Paradise is togetherness and harmony in the midst of the chaos out of which Paradise comes by orders of God, so the cross is the gateway to what we ought to embody and strive for in a world with little regard for beginnings. Truly the cross is Paradise. It is because in it the parts of chaos become an indistinguishable whole. It is the word of bearing the burdens of each other so that we will not only find rest in God. We will be in a position to represent the world to God as God's world. God is Paradise.

What then is this all about in everyday terms?

It's really Lena Horne's tears one night in Georgia upon rediscovering at a corner store someone who had been out of sight and out of mind for years. Lena wept that night. Her tears came from rediscovering the missing dimensions of her own being in a life that seemingly did not matter in the scheme of things. In Georgia Lena came back to innocence and to roots, to life without pretense. In Georgia she came back to her blackness to relearn once more the deep meanings of creation and paradise. She came home to the ancestors and even to paradise.

In coming back I would venture to say that Ms. Horne taught us all a lasting lesson. It is the fact that while the Divine One recognizes distinctions in our personal carriage and the issues we are forced by circumstances to confront, the Divine Being brings us back to the hopes of basics. That is, we all come to see eventually that our fixations and flirtations are not that important in the end. We come back. We enter the very gate we disowned.

What is this all about?

I can only tell you in bee terms, for bees do tell us about the procession of friendship God intends and about the nature of things touching things. As innocent as bees seem in making their rounds in the spring, they are carriers of the resurrection of life. On their bodies and legs they take pollen from the stamen of the male flower to the pistil of the female one. They ensure the joining of nature's hands whereas otherwise the process would be left to chance. Bees have not changed in their joyous reminder of what God is like and what God desires of us. They seem to know how to make life work. They not only know how to carry the load of others; they know how to bear burdens of a larger world.

We are not bees but humans. Yet by their act of mercy and compassion we are directed. We are directed to look back to our first parents and from that foundation to get in touch with our real purpose in life. From there it is quite possible to find the impetus to keep rather public through the channel of our spirituality and the Church what God requires of us as we seek to distinguish our charting of the world from the course it has followed in recent years. From the sacred window of creation all that inveighs against the sacredness of life and creation is challenged, and it is there we rediscover our duty of moving beyond compromised corners by becoming authentic witnesses.

In speaking of structures and undertakings that do not matter in the end (such as pursuits in circumcision and noncircumcision), in the letter to the Galatians Paul the apostle urged us also to move beyond the political trappings of context and culture to embrace the human condition as primal. Martin Luther King, Jr., was in the same stream when in *Stride Toward Freedom* he told of putting aside his concerns for a safe and secure future in the face of mounting threats to his person and family to do God's will. For this prophet things of God were necessary. The spirit of prophecy became guide because prophecy itself belongs to the foundation. It is challenged and guided by its directives. This could only be because at the foundation we desire to rediscover, reinvent, and execute on what belongs to a redeemed life and community directed by the foundation. For it is there we find the beginning, it is there we find our reason for being, and it is there we find direction for what we hope to be and for what we want our world to be. It is also there that we find the Lord.

8

When Sorrow
Follows Celebration . . .

RICHARD W. WILLS, SR.

And when they had sung a hymn, they went
out to the Mount of Olives.
Matthew 26:30 KJV

D oes the date April 3, 1968, ring a bell? Perhaps not,
but for the hundreds of disenfranchised African
Americans who were employed by the Memphis
Sanitation Department, it is a date that they shall never forget.
It was a cool, inclement, spring night in Memphis, Tennessee.
It was as though nature had altered its otherwise moonlit sky to
mirror the calloused social conditions that had become the
catalyst for their mass meeting that drab, stormy night.

And meet they did! No storm cloud could hinder the
assembled crowd weary of the unbalanced scales of social
inequality. They gathered with hearts hopeful of hearing heaven's herald. They had long heard the voices of paternalistic
appeasement and political gradualism, now only the voice of a
prophet could address the despair created by their current

Richard W. Wills, Sr., was born in New York and reared there and in Germany. He was baptized, licensed, and ordained as a deacon and minister by the Reverend Dr. Samuel B. Joubert, Sr., at the Community Baptist Church, Bayside, N.Y. He has received degrees in several fields, including architecture, and has pastored a number of churches. Dr. Wills served as pastor of Dexter Avenue King Memorial Baptist Church from 1992–1995. He then served as the assistant pastor of the Canaan Baptist Church of Christ under the senior pastoral leadership of Dr. Wyatt T. Walker. Dr. Wills now lives in Mechanicsville, Virginia, and works with the architectural firm of Kelso and Easter while pursuing his Ph.D. in Religious Ethics.

socio-political dilemma. As torrential rain beat upon the windows of the Memphis Masonic Temple, a fatigued Martin Luther King, Jr., approached the lectern saying, "God sent us here to say to you [Memphis] that you're not treating his children right." By the time he concluded his famous "I've been to the Mountaintop" speech, the audience was standing upon their feet with a renewed determination to see their just cause through. It was shoutin' time. It was a night of celebration. Advocacy had come amidst the storm to strengthen their resolve. But as hate would have it, their celebration was short-lived. Within twenty-four hours, the voice of their advocate was vanquished by an assassin's bullet. Sorrow fell heavily on the heels of their hope-filled celebration.

In many ways our Lord's Table stands as a symbol of life's brightest prospect and life's most brazen scheme. Much like April 4, 1968, one comes quickly on the heels of the other. There is a seemingly seamless transition of one experience into the other. There is no space, no pause, no time to catch one's breath, no *selah*, nothing but an uninterrupted flow of celebration spilling over into speechless sorrow. That's what occurred in Memphis, and that's what occurred the night of our Lord's Last Supper.

At the outset Jesus and His disciples were celebrating an occasion that spoke of life's bright side. This was the eve of the Passover meal. Jerusalem was once again bustling with Jews of the Diaspora that had gathered from the four corners of the earth to celebrate their God granting emancipation from Pharaoh's bondage. They got together to share an annual meal commemorating God's design to let death and destruction pass over their oppressed ancestors while afflicting the oppressor till the doors of deliverance swung wide open.

Folk of every walk and way were in Jerusalem to remember when! Rome may have been seated on the earthly throne that night, but heaven's hope was in the air as they sang, "Go down Moses, way down to Egypt land, and when ya get there, tell ol' Pharaoh to let my people go."

To be sure, there was some talk of death and departure in the Upper Room as well. As Jesus broke the bread and poured the wine He mentioned that these were symbols of His death and departure. Had Jesus received additional death threats as a result of his confrontation with the Temple officials, the disciples must have thought. Who has Jesus offended now? Would they really kill him? What a horrible thought, a thought that would just have to wait for some other day, some distant day. They figured they'd cross that bridge when they got to it, if ever. After all, they were celebrating Passover in the company of their conquering King and the shouts of "Free at last, free at last, thank God Almighty we are free at last" seemed apropos. Alas, they could envision the dawn of their brand new day, a day beyond the slings and arrows of Rome's outrageous injustice. This Supper, for them, represented a hymn singin', hand clappin', foot pattin' time. It's no wonder that they concluded their meal with the singing of a soul-stirring hymn. But true to life, heartache and headache and every other imaginable form of hardship comes, even on the heels of a hearty hallelujah, it comes!

And when they had sung a hymn they went out to the Mount of Olives. Did you get that? In any other context that line would represent a move from glory to glory, a continuation of celebration. The hymn would have represented the prelude to higher praise, a devotional period before the call to worship. They were going from the upper room to the mountaintop, and all of

them knew the value of worshipping on the mountain. Historically, God always met folk on the mountain, from Moses to
Malachi. This mountain, the Mount of Olives, ascended to the
heavens. It was "a stones throw" east of Jerusalem. It rose some
two hundred feet above Jerusalem's temple so that travelers
could view the Holy City as they approached it.

And tucked away in a western slope overlooking Jerusalem
was a cozy prayer place called Gethsemane. That's where Jesus
and His disciples were headed. It's still there! Twenty-first
century travelers from around the globe continue to converge
on this ancient garden, and they are just as overwhelmed by its
tranquility and beauty as travelers were two thousand years ago.

But there was little tranquility after the hymn the night of
this "Last Supper." While Jerusalem celebrated its indepen-
dence, and listened to liberation lectures and declarations of
deliverance, Christ made His way to a moonlit garden to come
to grips with His impending incarceration and execution.
Imagine that the whole community was singing freedom songs
as the foes of freedom escorted Jesus back to Jerusalem in
chains. As armed guards cruelly led Jesus through dim back-
alleys to Caiaphas, then to Pilate, to Herod, and then back to
Pilate for sentencing, I imagine Jesus could hear hopeful pilgrims singing "Ain't gonna let nobody turn me round, turn me
round." What a paradoxical footnote to their freedom celebration!

And this, I'm afraid, is America's inconsistent record. I love
this nation, and I pray that God will always bless my place of
birth, but as the star-spangled banner yet waves, this nation
must truly come to grips with the fact that while proclamations
were being signed, and while freedom bells were ringing, chain-
clad children of God were wondering why these same rights to

life, liberty and the pursuit of happiness did not make their way from the courthouse to the cotton fields. While fireworks burst in starry skies over plantation fields, they laid upon straw mats wondering "where's our freedom festival?"

To be historically correct, if we sing the *Battle Hymn of the Republic* with one breath we must then sing James Weldon Johnson's *National Negro Hymn* with the next, because "Glory hallelujah His truth is marching on" has a footnote that reads, "Stony the road we trod, bitter the chastening rod, felt in the days when hope unborn had died." It is a historical commentary on sorrow's painful and paradoxical relationship to celebration, one that persons of goodwill should always be mindful of, particularly in this day of unparalleled prosperity. One must never forget that while some on Wall Street are shouting "glory hallelujah" other less conspicuous crowds are wondering, "What ever happened to the trickle of the 'Trickle Down Theory?' What ever happened to the 'Thousand Points of Light?' What ever happened to all the rhetoric of a 'Kinder Gentler Nation?' Why was the long-awaited birth of our hope aborted so soon?"

At times, only faith can ultimately answer life's stubborn facts. If ever the church universal needed to exercise its role as friend and advocate to the world's hurting, it is at this moment in this millennium. Celebration, it seems, is the word by which secular and sacred life is most defined these days. Few aspects of church life seem as central to church growth as the congregation's ability to excel in the arena of worship and praise. And while I would be the last to discourage authentic worship, I would caution the church of the danger in neglecting to balance prayer and praise with a levelheaded pondering of what's going on in the world about us and what we are doing about it.

Make no mistake, it was no coincidence that Christ admonished those closest to Him to *"watch* and pray." In other words, get a good look at the landscape and then pray. There is something to be said about the value in *"surveying"* the landscape *before "kneeling"* upon it. I sometimes wonder what the church would witness if she seriously surveyed the global landscape. I wonder what she would see on the horizon of this 21st century. What's going on in life's dimly lit back alleys in this day of so-called enlightened self-interest, as an unsuspecting generation barely born celebrates the hope of a better today and a brighter tomorrow?

The Church has already celebrated through at least two decades of decisive affirmative-action repeals, troubling shifts in public education and healthcare policies, the expansion of dysfunctional families, painful police brutality and racial profiling. We continue to celebrate, despite the construct of an unprecedented prison system, the erosion of our environment, the perpetuation of suffering in Third World Nations, and a growing satisfaction with Segregated Sundays, in lieu of courageous attempts toward the creation of a Beloved Community. We celebrate beneath the weight of countless reports suggesting that something is going on in Jerusalem with little or no ecclesiastical reaction to the troubling "writ on the wall." It is not difficult to celebrate *not* knowing. In that sense "ignorance is bliss."

Celebration comes easy *not* knowing the doctor's troubling report, *not* knowing the nearness of ruptured relationships, failed finances, faltering friendships, and all else that comes to frustrate faith. Could it be that we've become so provincial in our praise that we've lost sight of what's going on in the world beyond stained glass windows, padded pews, and ornate wooden doors, or, worse yet, are we simply more unconcerned than uninformed?

Make no mistake, Jesus was neither unconcerned nor uninformed, and as such His celebration was authentically timed. When He raised that hymn He knew where He was going and why He was going there. Judas and his band of extremists did not catch Christ in the garden by surprise. He celebrates with the raising of a hymn knowing! With eyes wide open to the bitter facts of betrayal, denial, desertion and even death, He celebrates. Sorrow is on its way, Judas has betrayed the Kingdom, Calvary is calling, and yet He sang a song not grounded in earthly inspiration. As He departs the upper room He sings a Zion song, a song in the key of kingdom tide. Biblical scholars believe that Jesus left the upper room singing, "The Lord is on my side I will not fear; what can man do unto me? . . . O give thanks unto the Lord; for He is good: for His mercy endureth forever."

How does one sing that kind of song knowing that their transition is from hymn-singing to a place where we find ourselves praying "My God, my God, Why . . .?" What is it that makes sorrow give way to this transcendent quality, despite the certainty of disappointment? What is it that creates this buoyant hope that cannot be drowned despite the storm-tossed waves and treacherous undercurrents?

Perhaps it has something to do with an insightful discovery our ancestors of African descent made when they sang, "I'm so glad . . . trouble don't last always" amidst overwhelming odds and unimaginable suffering!

When the *Church* through the efforts of spirit-led abolitionists, missionaries and activist pastors had done all that it could, it then knew that the God of the oppressed would do the rest.

They celebrated knowing what James Russell Lowell knew when he wrote,

> Truth forever on the scaffold
> wrong forever on the throne,
> yet that scaffold sways the future
> for beyond the dim unknown,
> standeth God in the shadow
> keeping watch over his own.

That's the time to celebrate! That's the time to shout! That's the time to rejoice! When we've done all that human heads, hands, and hearts can do to fulfill heaven's agenda on earth *knowing* that God will do the rest! That's a good time to celebrate despite sorrow's knock at the door. By faith Christ celebrates knowing that He had done all He could to commission the Twelve. He celebrates knowing that the road to Calvary is the same road that leads to redemption. It is not the road to defeat but to dignity, it is not just a road to tragedy but also to triumph. Authentic celebration can't help but grow out of an abiding faith in a loving all-powerful God who—as my grandparents would say—can do anything but fail, particularly when we have done what we could, while we could, with what we had!

I recently had a conversation with Elder Adel Green, Jr., who was present the day Martin Luther King, Jr., preached his former chief of staff's installation at Canaan Baptist Church in Harlem, New York. Before concluding his sermon, King alluded to the fact that he would be eulogized within the next thirty days. He was assassinated in Memphis, Tennessee, ten days later. "I may not get there with you," he celebrated on the eve of April 3rd, "but we as a people shall make it to the promised land." King celebrated knowing!

And praise God, there is still sufficient cause to celebrate. Despite danger and death faith always sees light beyond the shadowy tunnel, it sees truth getting crushed to the earth and yet rising again, it sees that which is redemptive springing forth from the seedbeds of unmerited suffering. This celebration is the by-product of a theology that says the universe is so designed that sorrow can never have the last say! We celebrate knowing that the cross may come, but even the cross must ultimately stand in the shadow of a crown! We celebrate with the blessed assurance that our sovereign God presides over every sorrow and every celebration, working all of life's moments together for "the good of those who love God and are called according to God's purpose." It is a celebration that poses the "Why" question another way. Instead of asking "why me," faith asks,

"Why should I be discouraged and why should the shadows come?

"Why should my heart feel lonely and long for heaven and home?

"When Jesus is my portion. A constant friend is He.

"His eye is on the sparrow and I know that He's watching me.

"[So, I'll celebrate] because I'm happy.

"[I'll celebrate] because I'm free.

"His eye is on the sparrow and I know he's watching me.

"So . . ."

9

Setting the Captives Free:
Giving Through Holistic Service

MICHAEL F. THURMAN

The Spirit of the Sovereign Lord is on me, because He has
anointed me to preach the good news to the poor. He has
sent me to bind up the brokenhearted, to proclaim freedom
for the captives and release from darkness for the prisoners,
to proclaim the year of the Lord's favor . . .

Isaiah 61:1-4

I sincerely hope that all of you had a joyous New Year's
celebration this past week! A number of you turned out for
the Watch Night's services here at church on Thursday
night. This watch meeting service was a significant one as this
marked the last Watch Night service in which we could state
the year as 1,000 and something. It also marks the end of a
century, and the end of a decade. But I grant you that no one in
this building will be around when the next millennium com-
mences the start of another thousand years. Who will be around
in the year 3,000 A.D.? Now don't all of y'all speak at once, but

Michael F. Thurman was born in Montgomery, Alabama, in 1961. He is a graduate of Morehouse College (B.A., Religion and Philosophy, 1984), and New Orleans Baptist Theological Seminary (M.Div., 1988). He has served as pastor of Panther Creek Baptist Church, Mathews, Alabama; Village De L'est Baptist Church, New Orleans, Louisiana; Friendship Baptist Church (which he founded), Ames, Iowa; and Dexter, where he received the call in 1996. He is only the second Montgomery native to pastor at Dexter. In addition he has served as associate director of the Black Church Extension Division of the Home Mission Board of the Southern Baptist Convention.

in a thousand years not one of us will be alive! Several people have already begun to suggest that the New Year's Watch Night service for next year ought to be major, it ought to be big, it ought to be a coronation in which we celebrate together as a church family as we cross over into the next millennium. Furthermore, did you know, that on Thanksgiving Day of 1999, that the first worship service was held in this facility 110 years ago. Yes! We need to celebrate!

About three weeks ago, we observed our church's 121st Anniversary. My friend and colleague Rev. Charles Smith from the American Bible Society presented a lecture on the African American Jubilee Bible and on Sunday Morning he preached in our morning worship service. Rev. Smith challenged us duly during his time with us, so much so that several have requested that I do some follow-up teaching on the matter of African presence in the Bible.

It was during my search for an Anniversary Theme that the acute problem presented itself of joining this church's 121st anniversary celebration with the African American Jubilee in a manner that would make some sense. In desperation, I stumbled upon the Jubilee theme of "Setting the Captives Free" for the anniversary. I saw so much potential for this theme, for Isaiah 61:1-4 captures the essence of the struggle of the African American church in general and of Dexter in particular. Not long after I shared the theme with the committee, I said to Charlie in a telephone conversation, "Charlie, this is not a one-day theme, this is not the kind of theme to simply raise money on, it offers much more than that!" I said, "Charlie, this is the stuff out of which powerful vision is born." I firmly believe that the theme "Setting the Captives Free" embodies what history has portrayed concerning the significance of the church in the life of society, a bulwark force trumpeting the call for justice and righteousness in a society which has lost its moral compass.

The Spirit of Jubilee is a thread which runs throughout scripture and climaxes with ultimate liberation in Christ Jesus. Jubilee literally means a blast of the trumpet; it is derived from the Hebrew word yobel. It is commonly called the "Year of Liberty." At the end of seven Sabbaths of years, or forty-nine years, the trumpet was to sound throughout the land, and the fiftieth year was to be pronounced and hallowed as "Jubilee Year." This season of Jubilee was to be hallowed in three areas. First the Year of Jubilee marked a year of rest for the soil. There was to be no planting nor harvesting nor pruning during the "year of Jubilee." The inhabitants were to live off the bounty of the land depending only upon what the Lord would provide. Man, livestock, and land were all to be given a season of rest so that all three could be revitalized and renewed for another cycle of labor. In our time, Dr. George Washington Carver, the eminent scientist at Tuskegee, recommended that Southern farmers resort to crop rotation to save the soil from the excessive wear and tear caused by the overplanting of cotton and its effect on Southern agriculture.

Second, reversion of property was mandated during the "Year of Jubilee." This decreed that all property in fields and houses situated in villages and/or unwalled towns which the owner had been obliged to sell through poverty and which had not been redeemed was to revert without payment to its original owner or his lawful heirs. Thus debt release, or freedom from economic oppression, was employed so that everyone might be on equal footing and thus those whose lives had been burdened down by the heavy weight of debt could be released from the stranglehold of stiff financial obligations.

The third aspect of the "Year of Jubilee" dictated the manumission of Israelite slaves, many of whom had become slaves because of heavy indebtedness incurred in the attempt to get ahead. Every Israelite who through poverty had sold himself to one of his countrymen or to a foreigner settled in the land, if he had been unable to redeem himself or had not been redeemed by a kinsman, was to go out free with his children. Thus the "Year of Jubilee" was one in which freedom and grace for all suffering were to bring redemption and deliverance to the captives. It not only impacted the poor and the enslaved, but the entire congregation of Israel. These laws gave the Israelites new rules for promised-land living.

As we attempt to apply aspects of the Jubilee concept to our situation here in America and around the world there is much validity to be found in the Biblical practice. There is a certain civility and respect for all of humanity to be found in the principles of Jubilee. This is where we have lost our way; in a world built on power, wealth and greed, man has lost basic respect for each other. In accordance with Kantian philosophy, "We must always avoid treating others as means toward ends and seek to treat each person as ends in themselves." The proclamation of the fiftieth year as the "Year of Jubilee" was to place a statute of limitation, or a moratorium, on human viciousness. For if there is no relief from oppressive conditions, then the human spirit's powerful quest for freedom and dignity will seek creative ways to secure its own freedom.

In Luke's Gospel, the fourth chapter, Jesus, upon the inauguration of his ministry at the Temple clearly identifies Himself with the Jubilee theme. He proclaimed for himself, and rightfully so, the role of Chief Liberator, whose main job description was to bring manumission to those who had become victims of human viciousness and greed. Jesus identified with the despised and rejected of society, the underestimated, the under-represented, and the underclassed of society.

As we look out among us there are a whole lot of folks who are held captive against their will. The interesting phenomenon is that most of our captives are not aware that they are in captivity. Those held in captivity run the social gamut from the down-and-out to the up-and-out. Their senses have been deadened and they are unaware that they are no longer in control of their own lives. These are persons whose lives are in a dangerous tailspin. The accumulation of enormous debt has a way of doing that to people. Statistics show that during the upcoming year more than one million American households will file bankruptcy. The problem is that many fail to realize that they are in serious trouble until it is too late. Captives then become those individuals and institutions which have been held hostage by the immoral giant of greed, and all of its allies, as society attempts to conquer even greater heights of wealth and prosperity, and the subsequent power it brings. The captives represent both those who become the conquerors, the engineers of such a system, and the frontline players, as well as those who are left in the wake and turbulence of such struggle: the rogues and thugs of society, the pimps and prostitutes, the dope dealers, the homeless, the poor, the unemployed, and the uneducated. And on the backs of this latter category come scores of children. We then find persons in captivity from the White House to the outhouse.

The captives are those who have been categorically denied opportunities for growth and advancement within American society. They are the poor and displaced! They are young and old, black and white. They have faced obstacles everywhere they have turned! When they have applied for housing they were denied loans because their income was insufficient. They were denied jobs because they lacked skills and education. They have been denied health care because they were unable to afford insurance. They have been unable to partake in either job training programs or other educational enhancement programs because they could not afford child-care.

The faces of the captives become the faces of millions of children within this country who lag behind in nearly every social index. Their reading skills are poor. Their math and science skills are lacking. They have no access to health care. They come home to empty houses following a day of inadequate educational experiences. They are victims and perpetrators of crime. On the other end of the scale, they are our children who have everything society can offer. They are from two-parent working households, they have health care and adequate education and housing, yet they must be taught to deal with the real world of harsh realities of race and inequality. While they have so much to offer they still must prove themselves every day in a world which has written them off.

The captives also represent those whose lives are held at bay and thus plagued with a plethora of spiritual problems. They have been victims of abuse. They have experienced bad marriages. They have been victims of racism. They have resorted to drugs and other substances seeking relief from their pain. They are crying out to organized religions and other social institutions for wholeness. They represent those whose lives are squandered under the weight of spiritual deficiencies, the inability to generate enough spiritual energy to pilot the soul during crisis—lives which are deficit in a relationship with God. To be in bondage is to lose the ability to enjoy the freedom which life brings; it is to be bound emotionally, physically, and spiritually. Often these are represented by various addictions such as drug and alcohol, sex addicts, habitual spouse abusers, and the list goes on. Some on the other hand are hostages and have never lifted a bottle, never filled a syringe with substance for a quick high; they are held captives by low self-esteem, by low motivation, low ambition. These persons are held captives and prisoners within their own houses. This translates into low academic performance, low job performances, poor relationships, etc.

There has been great economic progress among African Americans within the last forty years just as there has been great prosperity within America during this same time period. More Americans have enjoyed the comforts of middle class living then ever before, both blacks and whites. However, African Americans are still held at bay when it comes to enjoying the upper strata of corporate life. Fewer than one percent of CEOs of Fortune 500 companies are African American. This level of wealth, prestige and power continues to be the domain of white males shared too infrequently with African Americans and other minorities.

As we enter into the next Millennium, Dexter must never forget that Jesus's Great Commission out of Matthew 28:19-20 has a direct correlation to the Jubilee passage in Isaiah 61:1-4. For it was out of Isaiah 61 that Jesus would find clarity in his own calling, as found in Luke 4. This radical departure from the norm is the foundation of the church. We must therefore seek to free our constituents, those who look to the church for a wholistic salvation, of the various forms of captivity which entangle their lives. As Isaiah so vividly states, our job is to "announce freedom for prisoners and captives." So often with the announcement of freedom comes the responsibility to develop the process whereby we can effectively announce that freedom, release, and escape have been made possible through the transforming power of God and his community of believers, the Church. Dexter, as we minister to the spiritual lives of our people, must also become sensitive to the physical conditions of our people, for often, only when we successfully minister to the physical conditions of people will they then begin to hear the message of salvation.

With this, the theme of "Setting the Captives Free" offers possibilities for some multiple-year planning emphasis. To make a dent in the great ills that even plague us locally can and will quickly consume all of our resources, not to mention the focusing of our attention on the much larger worldwide issues. The question then becomes how do we prepare ourselves to tackle such a mountain. The answer is one small step at a time. I am convinced that no matter what the height of the mountain and the variations of its terrain, if we take one step at a time we will eventually reach its peak. No matter if the mountain is Mount Everest or Mount Kilimanjaro, one step at a time is the key.

With this I firmly believe that this sacred institution's first step needs to be that of "Giving Back to Our Community Through Wholistic Service." One of the major criticisms leveled against the black middle class is that it has followed whites into the suburbs. Julius Wilson, in his book, *The Truly Disadvantaged: The Inner City, The Underclass and Public Policy* talks about the departure of the black bourgeoisie as having almost as negative an impact on the inner cities as the earlier white flight. The former weakened the tax base and the city's infrastructure, whereas the impact of the black middle class leaving the inner city may have even been more devastating because critical role models and positive success symbols were removed from many black neighborhoods.

One way in which we can assist in the great task of "Setting the Captives Free" this year is to "Give Something Back" in a multitude of ways. This church gives on average between $12,000 and $15,000 in benevolence each year. But the giving of money is not enough! Money cannot replace the human touch when a mother whose daughter is missing and has been missing for nearly three months appears on the church's door-steps with flyers in hands. Money cannot take the place of a role model who can inspire hope in the most dismal situations. Money cannot remove the fear that one has about letting go of the old familiar ways and embracing a new set of values when the old community looks in disgust as one attempts to rise above his/her condition. Money cannot buy these things! Money could not buy the redemption of humankind 2,000 years ago, nor can it buy it now! What the world needs and what Montgomery needs is the human touch!

Some time ago, I challenged every organization to adopt a missions project. In large measure my challenge was an attempt to ensure that we fulfill the Great Commission of Jesus in Matthew 28:19-20, but I also believe that it is an effective way to ensure that we engage in the business of "Setting Captives Free." If each ministry unit within this congregation would take seriously this challenge, I am convinced that it would change the perception of Dexter in the eyes of the community. People who are searching for church homes are searching for church families that are warm and caring. Giving back through our community is one way of changing the community's perception of us. That's what gets me excited about ideas like

Vernon's Place from the May Club and the Food Bank idea from the Deacons. That's what gets me excited about the February Club's adopting the Selma/Montgomery Tennis Center. That's what gets me excited about the Deacon Spouses' volunteering at the Resurrection Children's Center. That what gets me excited about July Club's willingness to work with the tourism ministry. That's what gets me excited about the Missionary Society's volunteering to work with Baptist Health Clinic for the underprivileged, and many other ideas from various organizations within the church. In time, it will be expected of each Sunday School class and every choir and every usher unit to adopt a missions project.

Critical to our taking seriously the Biblical mandate of setting the captives free is a need to move away from the old stereotypes that the community has of this institution. Churches that have the reputation of being untouchable end up in dire need of members. People tend to shy away from churches in which they fear being categorized and labeled. When churches open their arms to people from all walks of life and provide programs to meet the needs of people then those churches experience growth. In the not-too-distant past many people would select churches almost solely on the level of how much social prestige they could derive from those churches, or because of family ties to those institutions. A new generation has emerged and social prestige is not the driving force for church membership, but rather people are searching for churches that meet their needs. People tend to shop for churches today just as they shop for cars and clothes with a list of desirable features. When we become people-centered, then we will begin to see change and growth transpire!

Another factor must be addressed if we are to seriously set

the captives free. It takes tremendous economic resources to fund programs designed to meet the needs of people. For too long our churches have expended far too much time on the raising of money for operational expenses. We have allowed auxiliaries to become overly focused on the generation of money at the expense of doing ministry. For instance, the amount of time and energy expended in preparation for a bake sale that might yield $100 is a terrible misuse of human labor and capital. What would happen if we could ensure that adequate financial resources are in place and provide those auxiliaries a budget and have them focus their energies not on raising money, but on ministry tasks which will contribute far more to the church than $100. We must incorporate the Biblical concept of tithing into our church programs and teach our members to give on a consistent basis. And then all of our auxiliaries can focus on meeting human needs and we can move steadily toward the goal of setting the captives free.

Still another factor will be paramount in the refocusing of internal energies to engage in the task of setting the captives free. Church leadership must be mobilized and trained for the specific tasks. There is no substitute for planning and training. No church can be all things to all people, so perhaps it would be to our advantage to identify our strengths and build upon those strengths. What are our uniquenesses within the Kingdom of God and out of this uniqueness, what is God calling us to do? Not that in fifteen years from now whatever will be accomplished will be the result of some grand master plan, for this will hardly be the case. More than likely, whatever is accomplished will be the result of trial and error and, more then that, it will be by the Grace of God.

As I leave you this morning, I must hurriedly add that

setting the captives free is no easy task. It is a rigorous and demanding task! But with God's help and guidance, Dexter can become a major player in this effort. There will be some disappointing days in the process, there will be some days in which we will wonder whether we are on the right road. Anything worth accomplishing will be challenging at best. As the old adage goes, nothing ventured, nothing gained. But by the guiding hand of God, He will not let us down. In the shouldering of the task to become active agents in setting the captives free, we must learn to depend upon God. For as David says in Psalm 27:13-14 "I am still confident of this: I will see the goodness of the Lord in the land of the living . . ."

The role of the church thus becomes to act as surrogates so that the captives can achieve freedom in the Sovereign Lord. We can never take the Lord's place and become the healing agent; however, we can act as agents within the healing process and bring people to the pathway where they can have an encounter with the Lord. We can act as moral social agents by leading the fight for fairness and equality to help ease the pain in their lives, but only the Lord can make one whole again. But let us do our part to provide the framework whereby those who are captives can encounter God and begin the journey toward wholeness.

Epilogue: Part One

The Continued Cry
for Justice and Equality

Michael Thurman

s we plunge headlong into the twenty-first century, some forty-five years following the Montgomery Bus Boycott and some thirty years beyond Lyndon B. Johnson's "War on Poverty" Programs, an argument can be made that African Americans have made great progress in America. We have gained political clout, hold more public offices, and have a larger economic foundation that we did in the 1950s. More African Americans are getting college degrees, and we are finally breaking into the business community, one person at a time. In some areas, things look pretty good.

However, many scholars will question whether the illusion of integration and the dismantling of segregation made circumstances better for the African American community or worse. Ghettos still exist in the big cities, with thousands of black children born into backbreaking poverty. The disproportionate prison population grows worse, as a too-high percentage of black males daily enter into decades of prison time. Plus, the affluence gap is by all accounts widening. And I don't think anyone would be confused about what side of this gap the

African American community is on. So, there are strong arguments for either case!

I was too young to experience Jim Crow segregation. However, I know enough from history and from my elders to know how profoundly Southern culture has changed. I also know, as all aware and thinking people do, how much work still remains for the achievement of full justice and equality.

Prejudice and racism will be with us for generations to come. In fact, the world as we know it will continue to be divided in the ideological, cultural, economic, and class battles that we have witnessed all across the span of human history. That is the nature of man! But this does not free us of our obligation to be bearers of hope for the betterment of mankind. It does not prevent us from striving to eliminate the boundaries that perpetuate hate.

The quest then must continue, as the voice of righteousness must always summon the powerful, the ruling class, to the table and appeal to their consciences to do what is right. The prophets of our day have that moral obligation. These prophets may not have the charismatic power of a Martin King, nor the eccentric personality of a Vernon Johns, but their moral duty, whether they are leaders of churches with twenty or twenty thousand members, whether they be black, white, Hispanic, or Asian, is to remind the Pharaohs of this world that there is a Divine Moral Agent who is concerned about the welfare of all of his children, and especially those who are oppressed.

As we consider the nature of revolts and revolutions around the globe, we are reminded that the poor and disenfranchised of the world will not necessarily remain powerless. South Africa is an example, where a minority white rulership was eventually dethroned and the black majority that had been held in political and economic bondage for nearly four hundred years are now the holders of power. In Zimbabwe, President Robert Mugabe is in the process of doing what few reformers do—he is following through on the Marxist principles of redistribution of wealth by confiscating hundreds of white-owned farms and placing them within the hands of black Zimbabweians, or the government.

Exploring the environment of urban ghettos, one soon comes to understand just how potent the situation in America is. Urban poverty has worsened through trends including industry's shift to the suburbs, the collapse of industries, and finally the relocation of industry to cheaper third world workforces. These economic factors are coupled with cultural components such as the decreasing stability of the family unit, the decreasing impact of the church and other stabilizing forces, and the increase of gangs, drug wars, high unemployment, teen pregnancy, inadequate housing, police brutality, inaccessibility to quality health care, environmental racism, and many other negative ingredients. The ghettos are indeed hotbeds of potential and actual violence. A simmering anger and hostility is growing amongst many within the underclass of America.

These are injustices. Whether these injustices are externally or internally imposed, or both, does not matter. The fact remains that these are societal challenges that cannot be shrugged away, especially by the increasingly wealthy and remote upper classes and the politicians and bureaucrats who serve them. These problems will not go away unless we address them head on.

As long as injustice is prevalent there is the potential for violence and large-scale public disruption. Although much energy and attention has been given to the plight of the underclass, let us not forget the growing hostility of the conservative backlash. Moral leadership's job is to sound the alarm to prevent violence and the tragic waste of human life. Watts in 1965 and Los Angeles in 1992 (in the aftermath of the Rodney King beatings) both sent chilling echoes across the country. And just eight years ago (eight!), the Los Angeles riots spread across the conscience of America. This was the by-product of years of promises without delivery, the result of being ignored and tread upon. These were no different than the race riots of 1919 and other notable far-reaching displays of public unrest.

In 1992 I was living in Ames, Iowa, in a middle America town of fewer than fifty thousand people. Even there a riot broke out in reaction to the Rodney King beatings. This was not an isolated event. It was a public outcry that swept across the nation.

"Can't we all get along?" Rodney King's poignant question becomes the twenty-first century response to W. E. B. DuBois's prescient observation that "The problem of the 20th century is the problem of the color line." My friend and colleague, William Pannell, former dean of the chapel at Fuller Theological Seminary and author of *The Coming Race War,* warned that with the browning of America and with so many being systematically denied access to the Dream, America is rapidly becoming a boiling pot instead of a melting pot.

But we can avoid this bleak future! It does not have to be! Churches, as the trumpets of consciousness, must encourage every thread in the fabric of American society to do what it knows to be right and moral. Yet that is too simplistic a solution for this complex world run by greed and power. As one considers the function of the church within society, one weeps to realize that all too often churches are the preservers of the status quo, too morally impotent to sound a call to moral obedience and be taken seriously.

Corporations have begun mentoring minority candidates for jobs at the executive level and this is a good beginning. African Americans, Hispanics, and other minorities are beginning to rise to these ranks once reserved only for white males. Just as corporations were mobilized to exert moral leadership within South Africa by using their control of billions of dollars upon the South African economy, they must be called upon to do likewise in every place where there is injustice, for some powers only come to their senses when economic pressure is squeezed upon them. The Montgomery Bus Boycott was so effective because it brought moral, legal, and economic pressure to bear on the well-being of the city of Montgomery.

The church in general and the African American church in particular has as one of its major responsibilities that of the shaper of morality. Some church leaders disagree with the notion that the church has a moral imperative to act on secular matters. When I read the New Testament, I am convinced that the role of Jesus became that of Shaper of Morality, or at least, Chief Challenger of the Status Quo.

The African American church has moved, according to C. Eric Lincoln and Lawrence Mamiya, between six dialectical poles. These six poles are relative in that the church gravitates toward the various poles as circumstances arise, and thus the church's very nature is reactionary. Its dynamism has been brought about by its responsiveness to certain external stimuli and the nature of its response has been duly shaped by the individual church's history, its environment, its corporate outlook, and its beliefs that its theological mandate propels it into action. What follows is a snapshot of the dialectical poles that can be used in describing the African American Church. These poles are important to understand because they define the conflict inherent in every church decision, and help explain and predict future church decisions.

The first dialectical pair is that between priestly and prophetic functions. Here Lincoln and Mamiya refer to the opposite poles of the church's concern with worship, and the development of members' spiritual life. The vertical dimension of the cross concerns itself with man and his relationship with God. The opposite pole in this dialectic is that of the prophetic functions. This aspect involves the church and moral authority to address issues concerning the larger community. More often than not the prophetic function would involve a moral moratorium on some issue in which society has gone askew. The church would assume this role of "moral police" in order to pull the community in crisis not necessarily back to the center, but in the direction of the "High Moral Order." In other words, the church would appeal to the broader community to do what is morally right. As we entertain these dialectics it is important to remember that many congregations will rotate around both the priestly and prophetic poles as needs arise. The church may rest at the priestly pole until a community crisis occurs, when the church will gravitate toward the prophetic pole. The degree to which this happens depends upon the strength of the clergy and lay leadership of the congregation.

The second dialectic which Lincoln and Mamiya present is that between other-worldly and this-worldly. The other-worldly pole reflects a "pie in the sky" religion in which there is little concern for the day-to-day affairs of the congregants. More emphasis is placed on the afterlife than on the present life. A church with this orientation will be found dealing with matters of eternal salvation and damnation, heavenly rewards, and ultimate universal justice. The this-worldly pole concerns itself with affairs in the here-and-now. A church which operates from this basic orientation will be found dealing with matters such as the right to vote, lotteries, employment, housing, and a host of other relevant social issues.

The third dialectic is between universalism and particularism. This has to do with the church's understanding of the doctrine of the salvation of man. It is the basic orientation of the gospel message as applied to the particular favor that God has shown to the oppressed and to the African American community. A church that espouses the universal pole will desire the brotherhood of all mankind and will hold that race is of little significance in the Christian family, even in the face of great disparity, therefore oblivious to the present realities of life. While a congregation that gravitates toward the particularistic dialectic will espouse the belief that God is the God of the oppressed and will ultimately vindicate the victims of injustice and evil. The particularistic dialectic suggests a strong bend toward liberation theology.

A fourth dialectic proposed by Lincoln and Mamiya is between the communal and the privatistic. The communal pole refers to the role in which African-American churches have historically concerned themselves in larger community issues. These would include the many social ministries through which the churches improve the quality of life for their constituents. The privatistic pole explains the church's negligence to larger societal issues and its basic orientation toward narrower spiritual matters. The privatistic pole would almost go as far to embrace the church's withdrawal from the concrete concerns of life.

A fifth dialectic is between charismatic and bureaucratic. This centers on the age-old argument that the black preacher is largely a charismatic figure who alone makes all of the decisions, and encourages a loose-knit organizational structure. On the other hand there is the church whose basic orientation is to be more bureaucratic, to exercise shared leadership between clergy and laity, and thus is more likely to have a more efficient structure. Arguments could be made in favor of either model, but Lincoln and Mamiya observe that the African American church as a whole tends more toward the charismatic polar. The black church has basically been a clergy-led institution, which is not to slight in any way the contributions made by dedicated laymen and women, but to recognize that inherent in the African American tradition is this strong sense of duty and responsibility of the clergy coupled with a strong sense of expectation from the pew.

The sixth and final dialectic is between resistance and accommodation. According to Lincoln and Mamiya, this was a constant source of tension every black person and every black institution within American society had to confront. The church which revolved around the polar of accommodation for the most part sought to bridge the gap between the African American community and the majority community. It embraced a concept of social progress commonly referred to as gradualism, believing that the problems between the races would in time be solved. The accommodation pole was fueled by the concept that the church's main function within the community was to be the preserver of peace and tranquility, or in other words the status quo. The church which espoused the resistance polar was much more prone to social activism. This type of church held fast to the belief that the church was God's agent to bring about social justice here on earth and put up great resistance to buck the system and force it to realize and alter the systematic evil inherent within its being.

I mention these dialectical pairs to illuminate the complexity of the African American church. Like all facets of community life, the African American church is not a monolithic expression of community cohesion, but is rather a testimony to the rich and diverse tapestry to be found within the African American community. Therefore, as we talk about the African American church being the most capable institution, as has been reflected historically, to be the drum major for justice and equality, we must also understand that not all churches will be leaders in this endeavor. This is not to make slight of those congregations that are not as socially active as other congregations, but it is meant to suggest that we should be appreciative of the rich heritage operative within the context of community and therefore celebrate our diversity.

As we continue to be challenged by injustice, the African American church will continue to be the institution that African Americans look to for a prophetic word from the Lord. Here again, the black church must prove its relevance to a new generation of African Americans. Many, but not all, African Americans have made considerable gains within the last forty years. But the coming struggle will be radically different from the struggle of the 1950s and 1960s. The churches and people fighting in this struggle must adopt new methods to adapt to the changing face of bigotry and oppression.

Regardless of the manifestation of the new face of injustice, it will be familiar and must be defeated. The constituents of the black church will look to Dexter and churches like Dexter once again to provide leadership in this struggle.

Epilogue Part Two:

Dexter's Search for Meaning in the New Millennium

MICHAEL THURMAN

As we look at the function of the African American church within the twenty-first century we must address some pertinent issues. For instance, as our world becomes more global what will be the role of the African American church? Is there now a continued need for the African American church in a burgeoning global society and economy? What demands will be placed upon church leaders in the twenty-first century? Will the church be required to pay taxes by our government? Should the church be required to pay taxes to our government? Will churches become more vulnerable to secular lawsuits, and how do they protect themselves? How can churches and corporations work together to foster more positive community relations? How can churches work more effectively with government agencies to ensure that services for the poor and disadvantaged are delivered with a minimum amount of dollars tied up in administrative costs?

The list goes on and on.

The Dexter Avenue King Memorial Baptist Church is currently searching for meaning in the new millennium. It could be asked, what is news about that? Many churches are similarly seeking their way. However, Dexter is not merely another church. In light of its rich history and its identification as one of the major icons of freedom and liberation, its job now is to determine who we are to become *in light of what we have accomplished in the past.* We know that we have an obligation not only to our local congregation but also to the watching world, and we take this responsibility seriously. Having risen from origins in a slave trader's pen to being a torchbearer for the world, Dexter must continue to seek God's leadership and guidance with respect to our service to the larger global community. Given our unique position in American religion, what then will be our ongoing legacy as we attempt to provide light and hope to mankind?

As Dexter's search continues, it is necessary that we come to terms with our dual role as first and primarily an evangelical worship community and secondly as an institution with a far-reaching interfaith dimension. First and foremost Dexter is a church of baptized believers within the body of Christ who look to the Church to provide for spiritual growth and development. The evangelical mandate to be bearers of the transforming Gospel of Jesus Christ must never be lost in our search for meaning. As the very foundation of the church in the New Testament sets this course of action, the church must never deviate from the path that Jesus set. If it ever loses sight of this mission, it is no longer an instrument of God; we must quickly call it something else.

Secondly, Dexter is an international institution that has come to embody human rights and liberation, known all over the world, and frequented by tourists from many countries. Because of its unique place at the intersection of African

American religion and the American Civil Rights Movement, Dexter has an opportunity to lead in much-needed interfaith dialogue with leaders from around the world. This is a responsibility as well as an opportunity.

As I reflect upon the dual role of Dexter, it becomes apparent that God has uniquely prepared the institution to provide some great leadership. Will we rise to the occasion? This is always the real challenge, for the world has no shortage of ideas, only a shortage of those willing to carry them through. This is a demanding challenge, but one I am sure Dexter will shoulder, and with God's help will rise to great heights so that subsequent generations will continue to look to her for light and hope.

As we, like our sister churches, look ahead to the future, we address the above issues and even more fundamental issues directly impacting our survival as institutions. How do we keep pace with the changing times and trends? How far do our institutions go to embrace a new generation? How do we continue to attract new members when nontraditional churches and nondenominational churches seem to be ascendant? As Robert Franklin identified in his book *Another Day's Journey*, there has been a shift in the religious market. In the 1950s and 1960s black middle class worshippers flocked to traditional mainline churches—Baptist and Methodist—but since the 1960s this same group has begun to embrace Pentecostalism and a whole new movement of churchgoers have become affiliated with the Health, Wealth, and Prosperity Gospel.

Recently I was fortunate to be able to conduct a study, funded by a grant from the Louisville Institute, a program of the Lilly Endowment, entitled "The Revitalization of Historical African American Churches." A number of pastors of traditional churches similar in composition to Dexter were interviewed. Most felt that the traditional churches will remain the pillar of the African American community, albeit with some adjustments. The clergy felt strongly that traditional churches offered the best conduits by which to address problems pertinent to the African American community. In the new Word churches, the focus primarily centers on one's personal relationship with God and neglects the social conditions within which the Christian lives. The strength of the African American church has been in its holistic view of the salvation of man. This is not to say that the Neo-Pentecostal churches will not have an impact. The Neo-Pentecostal movement has helped mainline churches rediscover worship and praise and the gifts of the Spirit within the Body of Christ.

As in all movements away from orthodoxy, the dissenting faction or the emerging group challenges the orthodox group to make adjustments, and thus the gap closes which gave rise to the dissenting group in the first place. This happens provided that the issues with which there were differences are cultural, do not violate the body politics proper of the mainline group, and in essence are not theological matters. If the clergy interviewed during that study are correct, then the Neo-Pentecostal movement will help transform traditional churches as well.

To provide a handle on the perplexing matter before us, I want to again turn to Dr. Franklin's book entitled *Another's Day's Journey: Black Churches Confronting the American Crisis.* Franklin identifies at least six features which African American churchgoers seek in church homes. Every pastor and every church in America, urban or rural, needs a firm understanding of the churchgoer market, for churches like other industries are market-driven. Franklin suggests that persons seeking church-homes are searching for the following features:

Vibrancy of music and worship
Spiritually fulfilling and intellectually simulating preaching
Safety and attractiveness of the church environment
Quality programs for children
Programs for single people
Convenient schedules of worship services

These six items should be within the reach and grasp of every house of worship within the African American community. To what extent churches are able to deliver the above items will largely determine how successful these churches will be within the community.

In its continual redefinition and search for improvement, Dexter has begun to address several of the above issues. Our music program has made a tremendous turnaround within the last three years and this has had a profound impact on the worship experience. A major part of this expanded upon what was already in place and built the music budget over a period of time to make this a possibility. The choir was an invited guest for the Freedom Trail Gospel Festival in the Park sponsored by the State of Connecticut last year. This has served to instill a sense of pride in our music program and it has been a blessing to both the church and the Montgomery community.

The church has also placed great emphasis on its youth program as this is one of the entry points for young families with children. There have emerged some excellent leaders who are currently providing strong leadership for our youth. They meet once per month and do an activity each month. It is of utmost importance that churches not overextend themselves by taking on too much and burning out its workers as volunteer ministry partners are our most valuable assets. Because of the efforts and suggestions of our youth they have been instrumental in attracting other youth. For instance, we have a boys' basketball team, the Dexter Hurricanes. This team came about as a result of a young man who was not even a member who through his Sunday School class began to inquire about a basketball team for boys age 12-17. The Brotherhood of the church sponsored the team and this year after two seasons, they won first place in the league and third place in the tournament. I can remember being in the stands during the tournament and hearing folks in the stands cheering for Dexter. "Go Dexter! Go Dexter!" Although a small enough matter, it filled my heart with pride.

There have been other areas in which this congregation has attempted to address in order to remain relevant and a vibrant center of worship and spiritual uplift. And as in all institutions, we have experienced various levels of success in our endeavors. This is to be expected, for not all churches are called to be mega churches, but rather all churches are called to be the very best that they can be.

As I have taken on this challenge to provide leadership to this great congregation, I have become convinced of two things. First, no congregation will ever rise beyond the scope and vision of its leadership. Leadership is essential if a congregation is to continue to be a viable entity within the life and well being of the community and provide for the spiritual growth and development of its constituents. And the leader's commitment to aiding the church in determining the direction that God would have her to go is of primary importance.

The second thing I have become convinced is an essential

part of the success of a church is that the congregation must be willing to support its leadership as they search for God's guidance and direction. No matter how great the leadership is, if there is no support from the congregation then leadership will never achieve its goals. Behind every great leader stands an equally great force of followers who help the leader actualize the vision and goals. Without devoted followers, the greatest leaders will surely fail.

God is in the process of doing some great things through Dexter. No it will probably never be the center of a mass movement again, but there are other ways in which it can continue to make an impact upon the world for justice and equality. It is my sincere hope that within the months and years to come that Dexter will capture the essence of what the Sovereign Lord wills for its life and will rise to the occasion and do her part to bring about freedom and equality to all mankind.

Andrew Billingsley in his book, *Mighty Like A River: The Black Church and Social Reform* in the chapter entitled "New Time Religion" quotes Reverend Cecil Murray of the First A.M.E. Church of Los Angeles as saying, "The days of coming to church for personal salvation alone are over—congregations, are now actively pursuing not only personal salvation but social salvation as well." Dexter like most African American congregations in America is in the process of determining areas within which it can be most effective. We have asked that all of our auxiliaries adopt an outreach project. We currently have some twenty-two auxiliaries within the church's organizational structure. It has been exciting to watch these ministry units search for meaningful projects with which to become involved. Out of this initiative has come new energy and new focus for the congregation. For many congregations like Dexter, the challenge becomes how do we encourage and enlighten those who lead various ministries within the context of our churches to shift the focus from inward to outward. For many of our sister churches which face diminishing congregants on Sunday morning, the natural thing to do is to embrace a ministry approach which preserves and protects the existing ministry and this translates into a maintenance mode. Effective leadership must necessarily create programs and ministry opportunities that focuses the church on meeting the needs of the larger community.

Currently the congregation provides emergency assistance to over three hundred and sixty clients per year. These persons represent a potential regional market of future congregants. Their needs are varied ranging from the chronic cases representing persons who have an almost total dependency upon public assistance and other funds of benevolence, to those who are middle-class clients who have simply mismanaged their resources.

Plans are underway to open an offsite mission center called Vernon's Place. Vernon's Place will be named in honor of our nineteenth pastor, the Reverend Vernon Johns. This was a direct result of auxiliaries of the church being challenged to adopt a missions project. The May club (one of the twelve birth-month clubs initiated during Dr. King's administration) proposed the idea that we run a secondhand clothing store. The idea has grown to incorporate a youth computer center as well. The center will also house two tutorial programs, one affiliated with the S.T.E.P. Program (Strategies To Elevate People) which provides home work assistance to about fifteen elementary school children each week. The second tutorial program will provide testing preparation for high school students preparing to take the exit-exam. Alabama is one of the states within the country requiring that high school students pass a comprehensive exit-exam prior to graduation.

Plans are also being made to explore the development of what I call the International Dexter. We are looking at our tourism program and have begun to implement some changes in this area. Dexter is one of the top tourist attractions in downtown Montgomery. With the development of the Rosa Parks Museum by Troy State University, and the development of the National Center for Civil Rights by Alabama State University, and the Southern Poverty Law Center and the Selma to Montgomery Civil Rights Trail, Montgomery is positioned to be a major heritage center for those interested in African American history. We will open the old parsonage, of which all of Dexter's former pastors resided since 1919, for tourism in the near future. In the mean time, there is much discussion among Dexterites about the possibility developing a much broader ministry. Plans are being made to determine the scope and task of such an objective and how such a venture will be developed.

As you can see these are exciting times to be at Dexter! I trust that you have enjoyed this selection of sermons entitled *Voices From The Dexter Pulpit in the Post King Era*. These are the men along with some twenty others on whose shoulders I now stand. It has been a difficult stand, not from the standpoint of the congregants, for they have provided outstanding support quite contrary to popular beliefs about Dexter, but the stand has been difficult from the standpoint of history and the expectations which go along with such a historical place. For as a congregation we are a very private entity within the life and fabric of community, but we must be a public place and learn to accommodate a very demanding public's expectation. When private institutions become public it is indeed a challenge that requires the very best application of skill and thought. It is a welcome challenge, as it provides Dexter with an opportunity to reach out to an international community. It is my hope that as Dexter continues on its search for existential meaning that it will be gripped by a powerful vision, something that is larger than the two hundred and fifty congregants who worship here every Sunday, something requiring a much larger segment of the human family to be engaged and will thereby lead in the struggle to bring about Justice and Equality for all people.